# THE FORTIFIED HOUSE
# IN SCOTLAND

# THE FORTIFIED HOUSE
# IN SCOTLAND

## NIGEL TRANTER

VOLUME FIVE

NORTH AND WEST SCOTLAND
AND MISCELLANEOUS

## W. & R. CHAMBERS, LTD.
### EDINBURGH AND LONDON

NA
7745
,T7

First Published   ..   ..   ..   1970

ISBN   0   550   21210   8

Printed in Great Britain by
Robert Cunningham and Sons Ltd, Alva

# PREFACE

I N this, the fifth volume of the series, the author finishes a labour of many years duration—but a labour of love. The areas here covered include all of Scotland not previously dealt with—that is, the counties of Moray, Nairn, Inverness, Ross, Sutherland, Caithness, Orkney and Shetland, the entire West Highland seaboard, including Argyll, down to Arran and Bute, plus the Hebrides and the mainland Dunbartonshire. This great area is, of course, much less heavily populated than is the rest of the country, and in consequence has never supported anything like the density of fortified houses. Nevertheless, some of the most interesting fortalices in Scotland are here included, the West Highlands and Islands in especial producing their own distinctive type, usually of an earlier date than the majority of surviving Lowland buildings, and tending to lack the French influence which in the 16th century and after became so strong elsewhere. Save in these coastal areas, and especially in Argyll where the Campbells introduced an almost Lowland style pattern of living, at least amongst the landed class, the Highland countryside is remarkably lacking in castles. This can be explained by the fact that the clan chiefs and land-holders did not in the main go in for fortified dwellings, their kind of patriarchal (as distinct from purely feudal) sway preferring to rely on the protection of their clansfolk, for defence, rather than on stone-and-lime. This is clearly demonstrated by the fact that there are only eight surviving castles listed for all Inverness-shire, the largest county in Scotland, and two of these are in the Hebrides, whereas Argyll has eighteen. Again, Lowland Easter Ross has eleven, while Highland Wester Ross has but one.

As well as completing the area of Scotland topographically, the author has here included a large number of fortified houses missed out, for one reason or another, in the earlier four volumes. He cannot swear that, even now, every example has been discovered and described. Who knows, perhaps in years to come, he may unearth more of these attractive and exciting buildings to make another volume! But this seems unlikely. Every known source of information has been combed again and again, and an enormous amount of sheer physical searching conducted into every parish in the land, literally thousands of locations visited and inspected. But right up to going to print he has been discovering the odd and hitherto unheard-of example, a process which may possibly continue—for Scotland is rich indeed in this unique and valuable national asset, however grievously she still squanders it. The fact is that ALL domestic dwellings of the lairdly class, built prior to about 1650, in effect were fortified houses, and, because they were substantially built in excellent masonry and with iron-hard mortar, a surprisingly large number have survived, even though now often incorporated in later mansions.

A number of well-known castles were excluded from the earlier volumes deliberately because the author had decided to restrict himself to describing only fortified *houses*, as distinct from fortresses and purely military strengths, or indeed royal palaces. However, inevitably, it was not always easy to draw the line here, for certain castles which became military establishments had started as simple keeps and private houses; and some, though remaining the residences of great lords, by their size and strength became focal military points. There has been certain merited criticism on this point, and now the author has decided to include these large and semi-official castles, which were nevertheless privately owned and occupied—such as Caerlaverock, Threave, Hermitage, Crichton, Craigmillar, Doune and Ravenscraig. The true fortresses, never in private hands, however, such as Edinburgh, Stirling, Dumbarton and Blackness Castles, are still excluded.

In this final issue, too, the author has allowed himself a little more latitude in the matter of ruinous buildings than in the earlier volumes. So long as the main features survive, and the appearance is not very different from the original aspect, he has tended to include them, in the interests of having a truly comprehensive cover of the nation's heritage.

It but remains for the author to express his sincere thanks to all who have aided him and his wife in this prolonged endeavour —for it has been very much a joint effort; especially to the librarians of the Scottish Room, Edinburgh Central Library, whose patience and kindness has been consistent throughout; likewise to helpful members of the staff of the Scottish Home Department, and the Historic Buildings Record. Also, of course, to the owners and occupiers of these buildings themselves, up and down the country, who have extended so much kindness and hospitality. And, inevitably, tribute falls once again to be paid to the stalwart writers of McGibbon and Ross's *The Castellated and Domestic Architecture of Scotland*, whose magnificent work and untiring energy, in those days before motor transport, are a continual source of wonder and admiration; it is to the nation's loss that their great work has now become so hard to obtain.

It has all along been the hope of the present author that, as well as producing a comprehensive compendium of information, in a modest way, of Scotland's especial good fortune in possessing this widespread, meaningful, traditional and picturesque addition to the scene and countryside, these volumes might help to make readers aware of the continual threat to survival of this heritage of stone in the present age. Having withstood the ravages of warfare, time and the elements so successfully, it is sad indeed that they must now face the more deliberate threat of the demolisher, the roof-remover, the road-widener, the 'improvers' of all categories, be these town or county councils, industrial developers, impoverished land-owners, or just farmers who buy land and have no use for the castles and towers. And, of course, the ubiquitous vandals of the less authoritative sort. How many of the buildings described in these five volumes have in fact been swept away in the interim, it is scarcely possible to relate, without once again covering the whole country on a detailed tour of examination; but the author knows of all too many. Surely to our national shame, when no other country in the world has so rich and vivid an inheritance.

Fortunately, a certain trend is becoming apparent, in that not a few people of some means are perceiving the satisfactions and delights of living in such authentic and characterful houses, and are buying even very ruinous examples to restore and occupy, either as permanent or holiday homes. It is to be hoped that this will become ever more popular. If these volumes serve to plant a seed or two in the minds of readers which will result in the saving of a few more of these fine fortalices, then the author will feel well rewarded.

# CONTENTS

## BARCALDINE CASTLE

This handsome and substantial house of the late 16th century was at one time a roofless ruin, but has been tastefully restored. Beautifully situated on level land near the mouth of mountain-girt Loch Creran, four miles north of Connel Ferry, it was formerly known as the Black Castle of Barcaldine, though its walls, now harled and whitewashed, belie that description. Its plan is a variation of the favourite L, with the two wings slightly offset to improve defensive fire from the walls. A wide circular stair-tower rises in the re-entrant, facing south-east, and four large angle-turrets grace the corners. The masonry is pierced by oblong gunloops and small shot-holes, and rises to three storeys and an attic, with massive chimney-stacks.

The entrance is in the foot of the stair-tower and still retains

its heavy iron yett behind the oaken door, with an unusal stone shelf above internally. Externally is a heraldic panel displaying the arms of the builder, Sir Duncan Campbell of Glenorchy. The ground floor is vaulted and contains the kitchen and cellars, that to the west being the wine-cellar and having the usual small straight stair in the walling to the Hall above. The main stairway is wide, and the Hall is a handsome apartment measuring 37 by 19 feet, with off it, in the wing, a private room, panelled. Above is ample bedroom accommodation. The house, having been restored from dereliction, retains few original internal features.

Although built towards the end of the 16th century, by the famous Black Duncan of the Seven Castles, 7th Chief of Glenorchy, and forebear of the Breadalbane Campbells, Barcaldine was erected as part of a scheme to guard his great scattered estates, and placed under hereditary keepers. The other six castles were Kilchurn on Loch Awe, the principal seat; Achallader, near the Black Mount; Loch Dochart, on an island in that glen; Finlarig at the west end of Loch Tay, and Balloch, later called Taymouth, at the east end; and Edinample, on Loch Earn.

It was from Black Duncan's son Patrick, or Para Beg, second of the hereditary keepers, that the Barcaldine Campbells descended, and much excitement this castle must have seen in the stirring days when Clan Campbell was warstling its way up to almost complete hegemony in the Highland South-West. Para's eldest son fought with Argyll in the Civil War, and married a sister of the great Sir Ewan Cameron of Locheil. The next heir took part in the Campbell invasion of Caithness, with fifty Barcaldine men, when Glenorchy sought to consolidate his hold on that Sinclair earldom, gained in a financial deal with the 6th Earl. He failed in this, but was compensated by being created first Earl of Breadalbane. The Barcaldine family were much involved in the famous murder of Colin Campbell of Glenure, who was a son of the 5th laird, in 1752. In 1842 the estate was sold, but the old and abandoned castle was bought back again in 1896 by Sir Duncan Campbell, 10th of Barcaldine, and after some years was again made fit for habitation. The ownership remains with his descendants.


# BREACHACHA CASTLE, COLL

At the south-west end of the island of Coll, facing east across a wide sandy bay, this interesting castle, though long ruinous, stands in a fair state of preservation and is in fact now being restored. It is a fairly typical example of the West Highland castle, on a smallish scale and of comparatively late date, consisting of a square lofty keep at one corner of a high-walled enclosure, with flanking tower—though in this case part of the wall of enceinte has been incorporated in a gabled 16th-century house at the south-west corner of the enclosure.

The keep, four storeys high to the parapet, with a gabled garret storey above, stands at the north-west angle of the approximately rectangular courtyard. It is built of very rough local rubble, of both very large and very small stones, with walls reaching 7 feet in thickness and measuring 32 by 27 feet. The windows are tiny, and the parapet rises flush, with elementary drainage spouts for the notably wide wall-walk. There is an open round, and caphouse for the turnpike stairway, which rises in the south-east angle. Strangely, there are no fireplaces in the keep, and therefore no chimneys. A shute opens just above ground level to the west, from a garderobe in the Hall walling, at first-floor level. The only decorative feature is some dog-tooth carving on the lintel of the door from stairway to Hall. The flooring is of timber throughout, and the entrance was at first-floor level, reached by the usual removable timber stair.

The flanking tower to the south-east rises a storey higher than the curtain-walling, and is circular, measuring 14 feet across, the upper floor being vaulted to support a platform roof. Again there is a flush parapet, with spouts and wall-walk. The wall of enceinte

is interesting, with more features than the towers. It is rounded at the south-west corner, presumably for better defence, and the entrance is nearby, in the south front, guarded by sockets for a drawbar and hinges for an iron yett. Above is a corbelled machi-colation for dropping missiles upon unwelcome guests. The arrow-slit window at the other side is bevelled off, to give a wider angle of fire. This is the part of the walling which has been built up into the 16th-century gabled house, and the entrance must have penetrated through this by a pend. At first-floor level, near the flanking tower, is an external spout, presumably from a former basin within. At this level also, to the west, has been a corbelled projecting garderobe and chute, now fragmentary. There is another machicolation at the north-east angle of the round tower.

Breachacha was granted by Robert the Bruce to his friend Angus Og of the Isles, but frequently changed hands, in the clan feuding days, amongst MacDonalds, MacNeils and Macleans. In 1431, however, it finally became the seat of a branch of the Mac-leans, whose great island of Mull is in close proximity. The keep appears to be of early 15th-century construction, so presumably the Macleans built it. Later Coll passed into Stewart hands. Here visited, for a week, Dr Johnson and Boswell in their famed tour of the Hebrides in 1773. A particularly ugly 18th-century 'sham-castle' has been built nearby.

## CARNASSERIE CASTLE

This ruinous but notably interesting castle towers high above the main road from Lochgilphead to Oban, about two miles north of Kilmartin, a well-known landmark, now happily under the care of the Ministry of Works. It is not quite what it appears at first glance, however, looking like an early square keep which has been much extended and elaborated in the 16th century, in the usual fashion. But, like Melgund Castle in Angus, built by another churchman, Carnasserie is homogeneous, a deliberate copy of such a development, but in fact built all at one time, in the 1560s, admittedly on the site of an older castle. The workmanship throughout is very fine.

The five-storeyed keep has a parapet on good corbelling, with open rounds, on three sides, and a gabled garret storey above, now roofless. The wing extends westwards, a storey lower, gabled and with much intricate corbelling, stringcoursing and

other decoration. The rubble walls are well supplied with various types of shot-holes and very narrow splayed gunloops. There is a stair-tower at the north-west corner of the wing, with a moulded doorway surmounted by heraldic panelling and ornament, with a Gaelic inscription. The west front of the wing is enhanced with an ambitious piece of turreting, the corbelling imaginatively used.

The basement is vaulted, containing the kitchen and usual cellarage. The kitchen has a water-spout beside the great fireplace. The Hall, with private room off, having a fine ornamental fireplace, occupies the first floor. There has been a courtyard to south and west, having a segmented arch inscribed with the initials of Sir Duncan Campbell and his wife, Lady Henrietta Lindsay, dated 1685.

Carnasserie was built by the famous John Carsewell, Superintendant and Bishop of the Isles. His previous house was the smaller castle of Kilmartin nearby, out of which he grew, to erect this handsome residence on the site of the older castle in which he had been born, and of which his father had been constable for the Earl of Argyll. Carsewell was one of the most eminent scholars that the Highlands have produced, as well as a notable administrator. He published the first book ever printed in Gaelic, or any Celtic tongue, the Gaelic version of John Knox's Liturgy, in 1567, containing a compendium of the doctrines of the Presbyterian faith, this becoming the spiritual guide for Reformed Highlanders. He served as Rector of Kilmartin and then Chancellor of the Chapel-Royal at Stirling. He was appointed

Superintendant of the Isles, under the Reformed regime in 1560 and six years later Queen Mary made him Bishop of the Isles—for accepting which appointment he was rebuked by the General Assembly, but though never consecrated he remained titular Bishop until his death. His enormous diocese demanded correspondingly vast labours, but fortunately he was a man of great energy and herculean frame. A contemporary Gaelic rhyme indicates that not all Highlanders found him admirable:

> An Carselach Mor in Carnasserie,
> there are five quarters (45 inches) in his hose;
> His rump is like the back of a crane,
> his stomach empty, greedy and unfortunately capacious.

Carnasserie Castle passed, on his death in 1572 to the Campbells of Auchinbreck. It was captured and blown up during Argyll's Rising.

## CARRICK CASTLE

This is a strange castle, in more ways than one, to find remotely situated at the head of an unimportant Argyll sea-loch, appearing by its impressive size, fine masonry and ambitious features, to merit a much more prominent setting. Dating from the 15th century, and built, like so many West Highland castles, on a rock jutting into the water, it is oblong on plan with its north-west

corner bevelled-off in unusual fashion. There are other unusual features. The windows are vaguely ecclesiastical in character, being mainly arched, inside and out with rounded or pointed heads. More strange still, there appears to have been only the one real fireplace in the building, in the west wall of the Hall, though even this has been removed. In the ceiling of the ingoing to a second-floor window, in the bevelled-off corner, is a flue, ending in a small chimney-stack at parapet-level—which indicates that, despite the advanced workmanship of most of the castle, the archaic notion of having an open fire in a window-embrasure. There are three storeys beneath a parapet rising flush with the walling, and a garret storey above. A tiny courtyard crowns a raised portion of the rock to the east, or lochwards, wherein was the entrance. There was also a postern gate and steep chutelike access to it from the sea, here. The building, though ruinous, is still in a fair state of preservation though the subsidiary courtyard works are now only fragmentary.

There are two doors, both opening from the courtyard, one into the basement and the other directly above, the two floors having no connecting stairway. Both are protected by deep bar-holes. Strangely enough the basement is not vaulted. At this level on the south front are twin arched openings which look like windows but are in fact the apertures, with sloping sills, for garderobes above. The Hall, on the first floor, measures 56 by 24 feet, and has been a fine apartment. An unusual feature here is that three of the windows, as well as the door, have bar-hole sockets—something I have never encountered elsewhere, and presumably added for security. Windows to north and west have stone seats. There are two good garderobes. Two straight stairs in the thickness of the east wall, branch off on either side of the doorway, upwards, that to the right reaching second floor only, and leading up to an arched doorway in the south-east corner, with another garderobe opposite. The left-hand stair rises to the northern room of the subdivided second floor, and thence up to the battlements a storey higher. The parapet walk has been drained by the usual gargoyle spouts, but these are all broken away.

Alleged to have been a hunting-seat of the Scots kings, Carrick was originally a Lamont stronghold, passing in the early 16th century to Campbells of the Ardkinglas line. Robert Campbell of Carrick witnessed a grant by his chief, Archibald Earl of Argyll, in 1511. In 1532 Duncan Campbell was Captain of Carrick, and in 1562 John Campbell likewise. In 1685 John Campbell of

Carrick was summoned to Edinburgh on account of the young Earl of Argyll's invasion of that year. In the laird's absence his great lands were harried by the opposition, and it is reported that they took away 119 horses, 330 cattle and 188 sheep. In 1715 Sir John Campbell of Carrick was one of signatories to The Resolve, at Inverary, to defend King George's person and government. The property later passed to the Murrays, Earls of Dunmore.

## DUART CASTLE, MULL

This celebrated stronghold of the chiefs of the Clan Maclean stands on the summit of a rocky knoll at the point of a green peninsula jutting out into the Sound of Mull, about three miles south-east of Craignure, a prominent landmark for all sailors out from Oban. The building was long ruinous, but was restored in 1912 by Sir Fitzroy Maclean, 10th baronet, who thereafter lived at Duart until his death at the age of 101.

The first references to Duart Castle belong to 1390, which was probably the date of the building of the keep by Lachlan Lubanach Maclean, who in 1366 married Margaret, daughter of John, Lord of the Isles, and was appointed his Lieutenant-General in war. But the massive walls of enceinte is earlier than this, and is thought to date from 1250. This great curtain-wall, so typical of early West Highland castles, measures 80 by 65 feet, is 6 to 10 feet in

thickness and rises 30 feet high, where is is crowned by a parapet and walk, and pierced by later gun-loops. It occupies all the summit of the knoll, which falls away sharply to north and west, while a ditch cut in the rock protected the approach from south and east. A circular stair-tower, possibly of the 16th century, projects to the north where the wall is thinnest and in least danger from assault. A peculiar contrivance at the north-east corner is interesting, being really a massive projecting buttress of odd shape, designed to fill up a spur of the rock, so that no passage could be gained round it; and this is built up higher into a circular flanking-tower. The entrance to the courtyard is in the south front, originally approached by the usual drawbridge with portcullis.

The massive keep has been added to the west and north, measuring 63 by 46 feet, with walls reaching 15 feet in thickness, rising four storeys to the parapet and a garret storey higher. Photographs and drawings show that the parapet and two open rounds, also the garret storey, are restorations, replacing a similar arrangement. Though there is a modern doorway at ground level from the courtyard, the original door was at first-floor level to the north, reached by a stone forestair, which was formerly only approachable by a very narrow passage. The basement contains vaulted cellars and some mural pits or prisons in the enormously thick walling. There is also a 13th-century well cut in the living rock of the floor. The Hall on the first floor, now reached through an attractive modern Sea Room terraced out to the north, is a handsome apartment with a great fireplace with modern carved lintel, and round-headed windows with stone seats. The floor levels have been somewhat altered. Access to the upper floors is by a narrow turnpike in the thick east wall, interesting in that the door thereto, though internal, is provided with draw-bar and slot. The upper floors have been restored, and retain no ancient features. A doorway from the stair, on the south, is peculiar in that, though it presumably formerly gave access to the courtyard wall-walk, it is placed too high for this, requiring steps down. The keep's parapet-walk is very wide, owing to the wall thickness below—and previously must have been still wider, for though the parapet is now flush, an Ordnance drawing of 1748 shows the original parapet to have projected on individual corbels.

Ranges of secondary building line the inner south and east faces of the courtyard. That to the south, built by Hector Mor in the 16th century, has a range of four vaulted cellars, with two storeys above. The east wing, added in the 17th century by Sir

Lachlan, created a baronet of Nova Scotia in 1631, has a central doorway, its lintel inscribed s.l.m. (for the baronet) and dated 1633; and above, a heraldic panel. At first-floor level is a second great hall, having four large windows cut through the very thick east walling.

The history of the castle, and the Maclean chiefs, would fill volumes, and cannot be summarised here. The Macleans supported the Stewart royal house, and after the Jacobite risings the castle was garrisoned by government troops, after which it fell into dereliction. The present chief, who resides at Duart, is Chief Scout of the Commonwealth.

# DUNDARAVE CASTLE

Here is a castle which has much in common with Barcaldine in the same county. Both belong to the same late 16th century, both have fairly similar plans and dimensions, although Dundarave is somewhat the larger, both stand easily visible at the roadside, and both have been restored after periods of roofless ruin.

Dundarave is sited on a little headland on the north side of Loch Fyne about 4 miles north-west of Inverary, an impressive and attractive building, handsomely restored by the late Sir Robert Lorimer. It belongs to the L-plan, with a square stair-tower in the re-entrant and a round tower at the opposite or north-west angle. The walls, not in this case harled and white-washed, rise to four storeys and an attic and were well supplied with small shot-holes, particularly in the window-breasts. Angle-turrets crown certain of the wallhead corners. The door is in the foot of the stair-tower, guarded by a shot-hole and enhanced by fine carving and decorative work. An inscription reads BEHALD THE END BE NOCHT VYSER NOR THE HIESTES, with the Macnaughton motto I HOIP IN GOD, and flanked by the initials I.M. and A.N. and the date 1596. Higher is an empty panel space, richly carved with dogtooth ornamentation.

The ground floor is vaulted and contains the kitchen, with a wide arched fireplace, the vast flue for which requires the east gable to be very thick indeed. There are also two vaulted cellars, divided in rather unusual fashion by a vaulted passage, one being the wine-cellar with typical private straight stair in the thickness of the north wall to the Hall above. This Hall is a fine apartment, provided with a garderobe or wall-cupboard in the south-east angle, making use of the thickness of the east gable, and a private

turnpike stair up to the bedroom accommodation higher in the opposite north-east angle. There is a private or withdrawing room in the wing at first floor level. On each floor of the round tower at the north-west angle is a small oddly-shaped chamber.

Modern additions have been made, but these are low set and do not detract from the tall impressiveness of the original.

Dundarave was the principal seat of the chiefs of Macnaughton, replacing Dubh Loch Castle at Inverary. It passed to the all-conquering Campbells in the early 18th century, and is identified with the Castle Doom of Neil Munro's novel. The story of the passing of the castle is romantic. The last of the Macnaughtons of Dundarave married, about 1700, a daughter of Sir James Campbell of Ardkinglass across the loch. Whether or not the wedding celebrations were too much for the Macnaughton, he woke up next morning to find himself married to the wrong daughter, the elder—his father-in-law having his own reasons for the substitution. Thereafter, Macnaughton and his true love, the younger daughter, fled to Ireland, and the Campbells reigned at Dundarave. Thus local legend. The present chiefly family certainly is based in Ireland.

# DUNSTAFFNAGE CASTLE

This famous stronghold stands on a rocky knoll on a low-lying promontory in the Firth of Lorne three miles north of Oban. It was early a most important place, for here was a seat of government of the early Dalriadic kingdom, from whence the Stone of Destiny was removed to Scone. The present building however consists of a lofty and massive castle of enceinte of the 13th century, with 16th- and 18th-century additions. The walls of the original fortress reach as high as 60 feet, and are up to 11 feet thick, following the outline of the rocky platform; but the plan is approximately quadrangular with round towers at three angles and a gatehouse-tower of complicated squared shape at the other south-east angle. These high curtain walls, pierced by arrow-slit windows and garderobe flues, are surmounted by a parapet and walk, in the usual fashion, and enclose a courtyard on the crown of the rock, uneven of level and having a well bored in its centre.

The main later development has centred on the gatehouse tower, where is the entrance, 15 feet above ground, reached formerly by a drawbridge and now by a stone forestair. The original doorway was by a pointed arch 10 feet wide, but this was reduced to a smaller arch and then a square-headed door, with bar-hole. This opened on to an entrance passage beneath the

tower, with a small guardroom to the right. Parallel with this passage was a narrow vaulted chamber with two loopholes into the passage, and a squint to watch the doorway. Built above this is the 16th-century house, later restored, of two storeys and an attic, with a conical-roofed stair-turret to the east, which rises above the main walling. Directly opposite, across the courtyard, was the early keep, of three storeys, now ruinous, circular outside but squared within, and built on the highest point of the rock. The north-east round tower was similar, but strangely has no access save from the battlements. There have been additional buildings along the north and east curtain-walls, wherein were kitchens and domestic offices. There were 18th-century additions of two storeys along the north wall, with an outside stone stair, dated 1725 with the initials AE. C. and L. C.

The castle is now in the hands of the Ministry of Works.

Dunstaffnage has had a stirring history. Bruce besieged it in 1308:

> That stoute wes, stark and bauld,
> Till Dunstaffnych rycht sturdely
> A sege set.

Bruce granted a charter as Constable of the castle to Sir Archibald Campbell. David the Second dated a charter from here, and in 1455 the 9th and last Earl of Douglas fled to Dunstaffnage when he had risen against James the Second after that monarch had murdered his brother, to persuade the Lord of the Isles to make war on the King. James the Fourth twice visited here, and in 1715 and 1745 government troops were quartered in the castle. The Earls and Dukes of Argyll were hereditary keepers, and the title of Captain of Dunstaffnage remains with the Campbell family.

# DUNTRUNE CASTLE

As though growing out of a great rocky outcrop. Duntrune stands on the very cliff-edge which projects south by west into Loch Crinan, and looks out to Knapdale and the island of Jura, about four miles south-west of Kilmartin. The castle, which has been restored and made comfortably habitable, dates from three main periods. On to the massive 12th- or 13th-century square of the typical West Highland fortress has been grafted a late 16th-century tower-house, with starkly plain conventional lines, steep roofs and dormer windows. The plan is L-shaped and the angles of the masonry are rounded, but are corbelled out to the square

just below eaves-level to facilitate roof construction. Some modern work has been added on the only side possible, to landward.

Access is gained via a little courtyard, the doorway being in the re-entrant angle, now masked by one of two quaint rounded single-storeyed porches. The interior has been adapted to serve modern requirements, but the basic structure has been little altered, with the bare stone walls retained. The basement is barrel-vaulted, and the old kitchen has been converted into the laird's dressing-room, the wide arched fireplace being cleverly utilised as a wardrobe. From here a small private stair ascends to the Hall above. Other vaulted cellarage has been converted into a modern kitchen and a bathroom. Throughout the house, garderobes and wall-cupboards have been made good use of.

This was in the heart of the Campbell country, and the Camp-bells of Duntrune played a prominent part in the history of Argyll. Duntrune was besieged in 1644 by Colkitto and his Ulstermen, during the Montrose campaigns, when after Inverlochy the terri-tories of their enemy, the Marquis of Argyll, were ravaged by the victorious royalist forces. It is from this period that Duntrune's ghost is said to date—a MacDonnell piper slain by the Campbells. This spectre was solemnly exorcised with the traditional bell, book and candle by an Episcopalian clergyman, when in modern times part of the basement was used as his church. The last Campbell laird suffered great loss at the collapse of the Ayr Bank, and in 1792 the lands were sold to the neighbouring laird, Neill Malcolm of Poltalloch. In recent years, Poltalloch House proving too large for present-day requirements, Malcolm of Poltalloch and his wife have made their home at Duntrune.


# GYLEN CASTLE

The site of this fine castle must be one of the most romantic and inaccessible in the land, unapproachable even for the West Highlands, despite the fact that it lies only some 5 miles south-west of Oban. For it is situated on the edge of a high rocky peninsula above the waves, at the very southern tip of the island of Kerrera, with no road within miles. From the sea, however, it stands out clearly and most impressively. Obviously, access to it was always by sea.

The building, though long a ruin, is in a fair state of preservation, and is sufficiently interesting for the excellent Messrs McGibbon & Ross to term an architectural gem—unexpected as this may be in view of its wild and remote position. Although it belongs to the popular L-plan, it is not quite so simple of description as this might imply. It consists of a main block and stair wing, the former of four storeys, with gabled roof and an angle-turret at the north-west corner, the wing rising a storey higher to end in a gabled watch-chamber slightly projected on continuous corbelling and reached by a circular stair-turret corbelled out at third-floor level on the west front. Machicolated projections are provided at various points, with somewhat similar-looking projecting garderobe flues. The windows are small, and there are numerous shot-holes and splayed gunloops.

The entrance is unusual. The doorway, with bar-hole, faces north and has a defended approach and a machicolation above. It leads into a vaulted passage which runs right under the main block, with a vaulted cellar on the right, to give access to a little courtyard to the south, shaped to fit the rocky site, and enclosing the re-entrant angle. Here another outer door admits to the foot of the stair-wing. This square-headed doorway has an empty panel-space above. The main turnpike stair serves all floors but the watch-chamber aforementioned. The Hall, on the first floor, measures 16 by 14 feet—for though tall and notably well-built, Gylen is of small dimensions. The Hall has a projecting garderobe in the west wall, with stone sink and drain. Through the jamb of the fireplace is a recess, checked for a door, which opens into the ingoing of an adjoining window, for purposes not apparent. Above there is a chamber on each floor. An interesting feature is the elaborate decorative corbelled-out dormer-window, at eaves level on the south or entrance front, used as a machicolation to protect the main door directly beneath.

Gylen was a stronghold of the chiefs of MacDougall, whose main seat of Dunollie still lies on the mainland near Oban. Obviously this little castle was most strategically situated to command the southern approaches to Oban by the narrow Sound of Kerrera. Here, for safety, was kept the famous Brooch of Lorne, the Mac-Dougall talisman, wrenched from Robert the Bruce's cloak at his defeat in the Battle of Dalrigh, in Strathfillan, in 1306, by one of the MacDougalls, who were then in opposition to the hero-king. The Brooch was stolen from Gylen in 1647 when the castle was besieged by General Leslie, and became the spoil of Campbell of Inverawe; but it was later recovered by the chiefs of Mac-Dougall.

# INNISCHONNEL CASTLE

This castle, considering that it is the original seat of the great Campbell House of Argyll, is comparatively little-known. It occupies a small islet in Loch Awe, close to the east shore about ten miles north-east of Ford; but it is not very readily seen from the nearby road because of intervening trees, and the fact that the building is much overgrown with ivy.

It is a simple early structure, approximately rectangular, another Highland castle of enceinte, consisting of lofty curtain-walls 7 to 8 feet thick, topped by a parapet and walk, and with square towers at the north-east and south-east angles. To the north of the castle proper extends an irregularly shaped courtyard following the shape of the island, with exceptionally thick walling to the west, and two entrances at the north end, one on either side, an unusual arrangement. These must both have been approached by boat—unless there was an underwater causeway, as was sometimes the case, now gone. The walling along the east side of both courtyard and castle is much thinner, and may represent rebuilding. The access from the courtyard, at first-floor level because of the rising surface of the island, is by a singularly narrow door, only 3 feet wide, provided with socket for a draw-bar. There is the usual central enclosure with the main range of building against the south wall, in which was the Hall, with the kitchen and its great arched fireplace screened off to the west, and a private room to the east. This last gives access to a small inner chamber in the

south-east tower. The larger north-east tower is unusual in having a smaller square flanking tower still further to the north-east, reached by a curious narrow passage in the thickness of the east wall.

The castle, though long ruinous and overgrown, is mainly complete to the wallhead, and deserves preservation. It is alleged to date from the 11th century, when the somewhat legendary ancestors of the Argyll family were first established here; but this seems much too early for the present structure. Innischonnel was the stronghold to which the famous slogan applied: 'It is a far cry to Lochow!'—meaning that it represented remote security from retribution. Though the somewhat misty Dairmid O'Duine is accepted as the founder of the family, the progenitor from whom the chief takes his title of *MacCailean Mor*, was Big Colin, who was killed at the Red Ford, in Lorn, in 1294. No doubt this castle was his seat. A successor was created Lord Campbell before 1427 and his grandson was created 1st Earl of Argyll in 1457. At Innischonnel, at the end of the 15th century, was imprisoned the infant heir to the Lordship of the Isles, Donald, son of Angus, who had rebelled against his father John, 10th of the Isles. The child was brought here by Argyll after the Battle of Bloody Bay, off Mull in 1484. He was a man before he escaped, but after making an armed invasion of Badenoch in 1503, he was again captured and imprisoned in Edinburgh Castle for 40 years. At what stage Innischonnel was deserted, and the Earls removed to the Castle of Inveraray—not the present castle, which was not built until 1744—is not clear. The present Duke held a coming-of-age party for his son within the old walls of Innischonnel in recent days.

## KILCHURN CASTLE

Well-known to all travellers approaching Oban from Dalmally and the Pass of Brander, this large and imposing ruined castle stands at the tip of a low-lying peninsula at the head of Loch Awe about 2 miles west of Dalmally. Though its rocky knoll is now partly surrounded by marshland, it would formerly be an island, for the level of the loch has been lowered by some ten feet. This was the original seat of the second great branch of the Campbells, the Lairds of Glenorchy, later Earls of Breadalbane. It consists of a keep of the 15th century, enlarged in the 16th century, and large extensions to north and west added in 1693. These are now much ruined, but the keep remains fairly entire.

The keep is oblong on plan and rises to three storeys and a garret, the wallhead being surmounted by a corbelled parapet with open rounds at the angles. The entrance is in the west front, and is surmounted by an inscribed lintel bearing the date 1693 and the initials of John, 1st Earl of Breadalbane and his Countess Mary Stewart. This door is the only entrance to the castle, and to gain the inner courtyard and the extensions it is necessary to pass through the vaulted ground-floor kitchen of the keep. Unusual also is the position of the squared stairway, presumably of later date, which rises diagonally opposite, in the south-west corner. There are small vaulted chambers on either side of the stairway, in the thickness of the wall. The Hall, on the first floor, is provided with only a small fireplace. The floors above have fallen in and are inaccessible. There are round towers at the corners of the courtyard, well supplied with shot-holes. The later extensions within the curtain walls to north and west, are undistinguished and have the appearance of barracks, built to house the Campbell militia. There are two great kitchen fireplaces here, no doubt one for the officers' mess and one for the men.

The property was originally MacGregor territory, but at the fall of that warlike clan, to which the Campbells contributed drastically, Kilchurn was acquired by Sir Duncan Campbell of Lochow, and passed to his younger son, Sir Colin, who built the keep in 1440. It was strengthened and improved by Sir Duncan, 'Duncan of the Seven Castles', around the end of the 16th century.

Sir John Campbell of Glenorchy, a cunning manipulator, acquired the great lands of the 6th Earl of Caithness, by foreclosing on vast debts, and even claimed the title of Earl—seeking to clinch the matter by later marrying the widow. He conducted a great expedition to the North in 1680, when there was much bloody fighting, tradition saying that the Campbells crossed the Wick River dryshod on the bodies of slain Sinclairs. This was the occasion for the composition of the well-known song, 'The Campbells are Coming!' Eventually Campbell failed to gain the earldom, but was created Earl of Breadalbane instead. He acted very equivocally in the early Jacobite days, and was much involved with Rob Roy MacGregor.

The castle was inhabited by the Breadalbane family until 1740, when they removed to the Castle of Balloch, later called Taymouth, at the foot of Loch Tay. Kilchurn was garrisoned by government troops in 1745.

## KILMARTIN CASTLE

This small but attractive late 16th-century fortalice stands only a short distance above the main Lochgilphead-Oban road, from which it is easily seen, just north of Kilmartin parish church. Now roofless and not in good condition, it follows a version of the popu-

lar Z-plan, consisting of a main block lying north and south with round towers projecting at the north-east and south-west angles. A small secondary stair-tower also rises part-way along the west front. The walls, which rise to three storeys, are of rough local rubble and there are few refinements in stonework. The shot-holes are numerous but very primitively constructed, the windows are fairly small and two still retain their iron grilles.

The entrance is in the west front close to the foot of the south-west tower, is guarded by shot-holes, and above is a weatherworn heraldic panel, its details now indecipherable. The basement contains three vaulted chambers linked by a vaulted passage to the west. The chamber to the north is the kitchen, the vaulting of which has now collapsed. There is a stone basin on the outside wall with a duct through the masonry to allow water to be led into the kitchen. The south-west tower contains the main turn-pike stair, with a small recess for guarding the doorway at its foot. The first floor, as usual, housed the Hall, with a retiring room off it to the north. There has been a large Hall fireplace in the west wall, and a commodious wall-chamber in the thickness of the south masonry. The secondary stairway in the small tower is something of a luxury in a fortalice so small as this. There are small chambers in the north-east round tower, and sleeping accommodation higher.

The parish of Kilmartin was always an important and rich one, in the Highland ecclesiastical polity, and strangely enough this castle was the residence of its Rector, just as nearby Carnasserie Castle was the said Rector's house when translated to the higher status of Bishop of the Isles. Like Carnasserie also, Kilmartin later became a property of the acquisitive house of Campbell.


# KINLOCHALINE CASTLE

Dramatically and beautifully situated at the head of Loch Aline, an arm of the Sound of Mull penetrating the empty tracts of Morvern, this small but sturdy castle perches on top of a rocky bluff where the Black Water joins the sea-loch. It was formerly in a much more ruinous state, having been partially restored in 1890. The building is oblong on plan, measuring 43 by 34 feet, and its 10 feet thick walls rise four storeys to a parapet and walk at 40 feet. It appears to date from the 15th century, possibly earlier, but the south or entrance front has been altered and improved in the 16th century. The walls are of local rubble, having fossil content. The corbels for the parapet on the north front are original and very plain, whereas the corbelling on the south side is more ornate and elaborate, with an open ground at each end, and a machicolated projection guarding the doorway below. There is a similar machicolation on the north side.

The entrance, at first-floor level, is now reached by a stone fore-stair but would originally have the usual removable timber stair. To the right is a little guardroom in the thickness of the walling. This floor contains the main Hall, with a wide arched fireplace to the north, over which is a small and fairly crude stone panel depicting a nude woman with objects in either hand. In the deep ingoings to the two west windows are straight stairs leading down to two vaulted cellars lit only by narrow slits to the east. This double access is unusual. Another peculiar feature is the recess opening in the south wall, in the floor of which is a pit, 7 feet deep and roughly 6 feet square, only partly arched over with vaulting, to form a sort of aumbry with a built-up window—the purpose of which escapes me. There has been a half-floor above this level. The main turnpike stair rises in the south-east angle, to the parapet, but above main second-floor level is a highly unusual and elaborate provision. A short flight of steps in the

thickness of the wall ascends, and then levels off to a narrow mural passage only 4 feet high, this in turn leading down a similar flight of steps to the south-west corner of the chamber. The reason for this difficult piece of building is not obvious, and I have never seen the like elsewhere. At second-floor level there is a large garderobe in the north-east angle, partly built-out on corbelling into the room. Above, there has been a garret chamber within the walk, now gone. The parapet is high, with small window embrasures instead of crenellations, though this may not be an original feature. There is a little fireplace here, allegedly to boil water or oil for pouring down through the machicolations upon attackers.

Locally known as *Casteal an Ime*, or Butter Castle, there is a tradition that its builder, a lady called the Lady Dubhchall, paid the masons in butter—which seems improbable. The castle was originally the seat of the chiefs of Clan Aonghais, or MacInnes, who were vassals of the Lords of the Isles and hereditary bowmen to the chiefs of MacKinnon in Skye—an inconvenient arrangement, geographically! John, of the Isles, is said to have declared, in gratitude for services rendered, 'My blessing on you, Chief of Kinlochaline! While MacDonald is in power, MacInnes shall be in favour.' Nevertheless, the same MacInnes, one of the Councillors of the Isles was treacherously murdered, with his five sons, at Ardtornish nearby, and the lands given to Maclean of Duart, by Donald of the Isles in 1390. Presumably therefore the Macleans built the present castle. Kinlochaline was attacked, its walls breached, and burned, by young Colkitto, Montrose's lieutenant, in 1644, like so many other Highland strengths; and again a few years later, Cromwell's troops repeated the process.

## MINGARY CASTLE

This splendidly sited and famous castle stands on a cliff where Loch Sunart joins the Sound of Mull a mile or so east of Kilchoan in Ardnamurchan, a position from which its lords were well placed to dominate those strategic waters. It is a typical West Highland castle, consisting of the usual high enclosing wall of enceinte, in this case 200 feet in circumference, 25 feet high and 6 feet wide, hexagonal on plan, with the cliff dropping to the sea abruptly on four sides, the fifth being guarded by a deep ditch and drawbridge. This original work dates probably from the 13th or 14th century. At a somewhat later period the landward-facing north walling was heightened and built up inwards to form an oblong keep. This in turn has been renewed, some of the work being of a very late date, but on the same foundations. Secondary additional buildings of two storeys were also contrived, within the enceinte to east and west, the outer walling being somewhat thinned to give additional space. A parapet surrounds the entire structure, crenellated in places, with the usual flagged walk and drainage gargoyle spouts. There has been some alteration here in the 16th century, to which period belong the open rounds corbelled out at the two southern angles. A semi-circular tower projects slightly on the east face, with arrow-slits and shot-holes. The windows are very small and infrequent.

The principal entrance was to the south, facing the sea, and reached by a long flight of steps cut in the cliff-face, from the chief's jetty. This leads to a very narrow doorway, only 2 feet 10 inches wide, furnished with an iron yett and an inner door with a draw-bar and long slot. Above, at parapet-level, are the massive corbels for a protective machicolation. The landward entrance, over the ditch, was in the nature of a postern, opening on to a narrow mural corridor.

Though now a ruin, the building is in a fair state of preservation.

Mingary was the stronghold of the powerful MacIans of Ardnamurchan, a sept of Clan Donald, descended from John of Islay, the Lord of the Isles who put away Amy MacRuaridh and married the Princess Margaret, daughter of Robert the Second. The Ardnamurchan chiefs were highly important in the politics and warfare of the West Highlands, indeed of Scotland itself, and their castle the scene of much stirring activity. It was here that James the Fourth made his headquarters during his campaigns to reduce the Islesmen to his rule, in 1493 and 1495. It was much damaged by Alexander of Lochalsh in the internecine clan wars that followed, and several times besieged by the Macleans and others. In 1644 it was taken for Montrose by the famous Colkitto, and thereafter used as a prison for a number of the early Covenant supporters, including three ministers. The castle features in Scott's *Lord of the Isles*.

## CASTLE MOY, MULL

Sometimes called Lochbuie Castle, this small and little-known but interesting fortalice is attractively sited at the head of the wide bay of Loch Buie on the south shore of Mull, about 15 miles south-west of Craignure. The commodious 18th-century mansion of Lochbuie stands nearby. This was the ancient seat of the Maclaines of Lochbuie, a branch of the Clan Maclean, who held the property for almost six centuries. The castle was abandoned as a residence in 1752, and when Dr Johnson and Boswell visited here in 1773, they stayed in a smaller house adjoining, now the stable-yard of the mansion.

The castle, though now ruinous, remains entire to the wallhead, and rises from a rocky mound directly above the sea-shore. It is an oblong keep, the walls of roughly coursed rubble, buttressed with a batter at all angles, rising three main storeys to a flush parapet, deeply crenellated, with a walk drained by a great many rough spouts. There is a gabled garret storey above, now ruined. Open rounds, which may possibly have been roofed over as angle-turrets, crown the north-east and south-east corners; while the other two angles are surmounted by a caphouse for the stair at the south-west and a gabled watch-chamber partially projecting on corbelling and having its own chimney-stack, at the north-west. The windows are small and sparse. There is a corbelled projection at parapet level to the north, and a chute from a garde-robe on the first floor, to the west.

The entrance is to the east, at ground level but only approachable by clambering over the naked rock. The interior was inaccessible, but the usual arrangement of vaulted basement, turnpike stair in the south-west angle, Hall on first floor and sleeping accommodation above, would apply. The building is said to date from as early as the 14th century, but basically it appears to be of 16th-century construction.

The Maclaines were a turbulent branch of a turbulent clan, and it is probable that this remote castle was the scene of many stirring episodes. Hector Reaganach was the brother of Lachlan Lubanach, from whom the house of Duart, chiefs of Maclean, derive. He received these lands from John, Lord of the Isles. John Og, 5th of Lochbuie, was succeeded by his young son Short Murdoch about 1494. John Og's brother, Murdoch of Scallasdale, seized the property and forced his nephew to flee to Ireland. But in due course Short Murdoch returned, with supporters, and making himself known to his old nurse at the castle, gained access thereto. Later he defeated his uncle in battle at Grulin. This may possibly be another version of the picturesque story in which Maclean of Duart, coveting Lochbuie, is said to have captured the heir and confined him on the Treshnish isle of Carnburgh, cautiously choosing as his housekeeper and only companion an old and ugly woman, so that there might be no further Maclaines of Lochbuie. However, after some years the lady was found to be pregnant, and though Maclaine himself was disposed of, the lady was smuggled to safety by a family of father and five sons, all of whom died rather than reveal her whereabouts. In the end a young man returned to Mull, claiming to be the son of Maclaine and this woman, and succeeded in regaining his inheritance.

Maclaine of Lochbuie, having supported Montrose, with his kinsmen from Duart, rode with 300 men to join Bonnie Dundee and distinguished himself in that campaign. It is only comparatively recently that the estate finally passed out of the hands of the Maclaines.

## SADDELL CASTLE

Now unfortunately in a bad state of repair, this picturesque and substantial fortalice stands on the shore of Saddell Bay, Kintyre, four miles south of Carradale, near the ruins of Saddell Abbey. Its site would once be strong, for the tide is said to have practically surrounded it. It is a large oblong keep of four storeys beneath a crenellated parapet on massive corbelling, with a garret storey above. The parapet is of unusual height, 4 feet 8 inches, and is provided with open rounds at the angles, these being projected on open corbelling to form machicolations through which missiles might be dropped on intruders. A semi-circular machicolation also projects directly above the door in the centre of the east front. The windows are fairly small and the walls have been harled. A forecourt lies to the east, entered by an ornate arched gateway of later date.

The moulded doorway, approached from this courtyard, is surmounted by a panel depicting the Galley of Lorne with the recut date 1508; the upper works of this castle, however, would appear to date from rather later than this. A turnpike stair rises to the right, ending in a small gabled caphouse at parapet level. This stairway juts internally on each floor, the walls being insufficiently thick to contain it. The basement, divided into two vaulted cellars, is some 5 feet below courtyard level, necessitating a flight of steps down from the entrance passage. The southern chamber has a private stair to the floor above, and would be the winecellar, unusual in having a garderobe and shute. The first floor is also subdivided, with the Hall to the north and a narrow kitchen

only $7\frac{1}{2}$ feet wide, to the south—though its wide fireplace is itself another $5\frac{1}{2}$ feet deep. There are an oven, aumbries and a large recess in this thick south wall. The Hall itself is comparatively featureless. The second floor has been divided into four apartments, three with fireplaces, and one having a stone window seat and garderobe. The third floor has only three apartments, the central one having also a large garderobe and window-seat but no fireplace, and the southern chamber very irregularly shaped owing to the inward projection of the great kitchen fireplace flue. These internal partitions are probably of late date.

Saddell was church lands, the abbey being instituted by Reginald, son of Somerled who founded the Isles dynasty and who is said to be buried here. His great-grandson, Angus Og, welcomed Bruce here in 1306 after his defeats at Methven and Dalrigh. In 1507-8 the abbey lands were made a barony by James the Fourth, who had taken over the Lordship of the Isles, and given to Bishop David Hamilton, who was granted a licence to build a castle. In 1558 Sussex, on a punitive raid from Ireland, wrote: 'I landed and burned eight myles of length and therewith James McConnel's chief house called Saudell, a fayre pile and a strong.' It would be after this burning that the upper works were rebuilt.

# SKIPNESS CASTLE

This handsome castle stands on a raised beach above the shore of the Kilbrannan Sound, opposite the tip of Arran, on the east side of the Kintyre peninsula some 12 miles south of Tarbert—strangely in a not obviously strong position. Though no longer occupied, it remains in a fairish state of repair. It consists of an early and typical Highland castle of enceinte, though with a still older nucleus, of the late and early 13th century repectively; with a late 16th- and early 17th-century keep rising at the north-east corner. The older castle's curtain-walls, over 6 feet thick, rise to about 30 feet in height and have a circumference of over 400 feet. There are projecting rectangular towers at the north-east and south-east angles, and near the centre of the west front. The entrance was originally in the south curtain, facing the sea, through a gate-tower provided with portcullis and machicolation. There was also a postern gate in the east wall, near the north end. The present arched courtyard entrance to the north is of later date. The parapet-walk along the wallhead was reached by a forestair at the south end.

The 16th- and 17th-century keep is L-shaped, and rises four storeys to a parapet and walk, with open rounds at three corners and a gabled caphouse above the stair-head at the fourth. There is a gabled garret chamber within the walk. The walls of the earlier castle are incorporated. The wing, which is so small as barely to merit that description, houses garderobes on each floor, and a wide chute to carry the flues therefor. The basement is now vaulted, but obviously this is an insertion to earlier masonry, and there is an arched doorway in the south wall, but no connection with the upper floors. The first floor is reached by an external stone forestair of late construction, to the present doorway in the south-east corner; but this again is an alteration, the previous doorway having been central in the south front. The Hall has no proper fireplace, but the ingoing of the northern window is fitted with a chimney-flue which would turn it into a kind of fireplace —an odd and primitive arrangement for so late a date, yet one which we also find at Carrick Castle in the same county. From the other side of this window opens a mural passage leading to one of the aforementioned garderobes in the wing. In the south-east corner is a recess, from which a straight mural stair rises to the next floor.

This second-floor chamber has been similar to that below, and here another window has been blocked up and turned into a fireplace. A turnpike stair rises hereafter, beside the wing, to end in the 17th-century caphouse. The third floor is entered by a pointed arched doorway, and this also has a converted window-fireplace, and its west window has window-seats. Both these floors have mural passages to garderobes. The garret flooring has gone. The caphouse however has a proper fireplace, garderobe and aumbry. It seems as though the later lairds of Skipness were more concerned with sanitation than with keeping warm—though larger living premises in the old castle of enceinte may have accounted for this.

In 1247 'Schepehinche' was the castle of one Dufgal son of Syfyn, and in 1262 the larger castle of enciente was built on to this by the Earl of Menteith, whom Alexander the Second appointed to hold the territory in the long struggle against the Norse domination of the Highland West. In 1499, while James the Fourth was bringing the dissident Lordship of the Isles under control, Skipness came under Campbell overlordship, and so remained.

# CASTLE STALKER

This well-known landmark of the Appin coast, sited dramatically on a small islet in Loch Linnhe just off Portnacroish, was long a ruin, but has recently been restored by the enthusiasm of a new owner. It is a tall, massive and simple rectangular keep dating from the 15th century. Measuring 50 by 40 feet, with walls reaching 9 feet in thickness, it rises in rude strength four storeys to an open parapet flush with the walling, with a garret storey above, within the parapet-walk. The spiral stairway ascends in the north-west angle, and ends in a small gabled caphouse and watch-chamber, which, with the whole garret storey, helps to create a dramatic roof-line. These upper storeys and elaborations were added in 1631; to this period also belongs the single open round, with shot-holes, at the south-west angle.

There are two entrances. The vaulted basement has a moulded doorway in the east front, defended by a machicolation above at parapet-level, and was also reached by a small mural stairway from the Hall above. There is a pit or prison in the north-west angle, reached by a trap-door in the foot of the main stairway. The principal door is at first-floor level in the north wall, now reached by a stone forestair outside, and also having a defensive machicolation high above. This access is interesting, for the original forestair reached only to the side of the arched doorway

leaving a gap, for security reasons, which could be bridged, when required, by a movable timber platform, the socket-holes for which remain. Later this gap was built up, when convenience over-rode defence. The Hall measures 31 by 21 feet, with a fireplace and a garderobe in the west wall, and one of its three windows having stone seats. Above was the normal bedroom accommodation. The small watch-chamber is enhanced with an unusually decorative fireplace. The chimney-stacks have notably high copes. A small courtyard extends to the south, the only available space on the islet, where the landing-place, reached by boat, is a few rude steps.

Castle Stalker was built by Duncan Stewart, grandson of Sir John Stewart, last Stewart Lord of Lorne, murdered in 1463. His father, Dugald Stewart, was the first of Appin—which word means the abbatial lands of Lismore. This Duncan was made Chamberlain of the Isles by James the Fourth, having greatly aided that monarch in his campaign to subdue the Lordship of the Isles. James is said to have hunted from Castle Stalker. Although Duncan's father was himself a son of Isabella Campbell, daughter of the first Earl of Argyll, the assassination of Campbell of Cawdor in 1592 caused a feud between that clan and the Appin Stewarts, which was to rage for centuries. Duncan Stewart, 7th of Appin, led his clan at Inverlochy, under Montrose, and it may well have been this chief who altered the roofline of Castle Stalker. The 8th chief fought at Sheriffmuir for the Chevalier, and the 9th aided Prince Charles in 1745. This Dugald, the 9th, being forfeited, had to sell the estates in 1765, the chiefship thereafter going to the Ardshiel branch, and Castle Stalker gradually falling into ruin. It is good to see it restored.

# BANFFSHIRE

## BALLINDALLOCH CASTLE

Picturesquely situated on level ground at the junction of the
Rivers Avon and Spey, between Aberlour and Grantown, Ballindalloch is a handsome and imposing mansion which has developed
from a fortalice of the 16th century. With later additions it was
greatly enlarged in 1845, in the castellated style—but still the
original work is clearly discernible, particularly at the western
side.

The early castle was on the Z-plan, with main block lying north
and south, and towers projecting to the north-west and south-east.
Later, in 1602, a handsome circular stair-tower was erected midway along the west front, rising a storey higher and ending in an
attractive watch-chamber, corbelled out to the square, with a
stair-turret in the northern re-entrant to give access to it. At the
head of this stair-turret is a machicolated projection from which
missiles could be dropped on to intruders at the arched entrance
below. A lower wing was extended westwards at the south end,
in the early 18th century, and in the next century were the very
large additions elswhere. The walls are roughcast, pierced with
sundry shot-holes, and the windows of the old work are small.
The oriel in the watch-chamber is particularly attractive, and is
initialled R. G. and dated 1602. The various roof-levels are very
diverse and make a pleasing skyline. The masonry of the chimney-
stack rising above the north-west round tower is itself rounded,
as at Harthill and Pitfichie Castles, Aberdeenshire.

Internally there has been a great deal of alteration, to link up
with the various additions. The basement is vaulted, and the
usual arrangements of Hall on first floor and bedroom accommodation above would apply. One fireplace is dated 1546.

Originally the lands are said to have belonged to a family which
took its name from them, the Ballindallochs of that Ilk. But as

the up-and-coming Clan Grant spread eastwards, Ballindalloch
came into their hands. There is a romantic story told of the building of the castle, on this site. Tradition says that it was to be
erected further up the river, on a more obviously strong site, but
that the work was continually delayed by some unseen agency,
the part built during the day being always thrown down again
during the night. At length, the laird heard a voice saying 'Build
in the cow-haugh, and you shall meet with no interruptions.'
What was then a marshy site was accordingly chosen, and the
castle rose undisturbed. A marshy site, of course, could be just
as defensively effective as a cliff or promontory.

This laird would not be a Grant, but another story does refer
to the later owners. The baron, of course, had the power of pit
and gallows, and it is told how one culprit, named Rob, earned
the laird's wrath for some misdemeanour. He himself disapproved
of the laird's justice however, and being a sturdy character
kicked out at his fellow-vassals and looked as though he would
escape. His wife, however, watching, spoke up. 'Och, Rob—be
quiet and dinna anger the laird!' she advised. The appeal brought
Rob to his sense of duty, and he submitted and died like a lamb.

In the early 18th century the Laird of Grant gave Ballindalloch
to Colonel William Grant, second son of Rothiemurchus, and his
daughter and heiress married George Macpherson of Invereshie,
in Badenoch. General James Grant defeated the French at St.

Lucia and was Governor of Florida, dying 1806. His successor, George Macpherson-Grant, was created a baronet in 1838. Their descendant is still at Ballindalloch.

## BALVENIE CASTLE

This fine castle, now happily cared for by the Ministry of Works after long being in a state of great neglect, is of especial interest in that it demonstrates the development of castle-building over a long period, in a clear and recognisable way. Dating from the 13th, 15th and late 16th centuries, it stands in a strong position above the River Fiddich half a mile north of Dufftown, readily seen from the main road.

From outside the courtyard, the impression is of great age and size, in that the lofty curtain walls of the original strength, 25 and more feet in height and 7 feet thick, are still approximately entire, enclosing a large quadrangle about 160 by 130 feet. But within the enclosure it is the 16th-century L-shaped building which is best preserved and dominates the scene. This forms the south-eastern corner of the whole. The first, or 15th-century, additions and alterations are mainly internal and are scarcely to be discerned. There has been much lean-to building of various dates within the courtyard, most of which has now disappeared.

The entrance front is to the south, and the contrast between the 13th- and 16th-century work is very marked; the former of massive well-coursed rubble, but notably plain; the latter decorated with string-courses and panels, and pierced by many very large splayed gunloops. A feature of this work is the great projecting circular tower, at the south-east angle which protects the south and east curtains. It has a tall, slender stair-turret corbelled out in its western re-entrant.

The arched entrance is in the 16th-century work, and admits to a vaulted pend. It is still provided with its very unusual double-winged iron yett, one side of which is obviously of later and poorer workmanship than the other. Stone porters' benches flank the transe, and a narrow guardroom opens on the left. Above the gateway are the Royal Arms of Scotland, and those of Stewart of Atholl, with the proudly practical motto, FYRTH FORTVIN AND FIL THI FATRIS—or, Forth Fortune, and File thy Fetters.

Of the main structure, the early work to the left contains a vaulted cellar and bakery on the ground floor, and a Great Hall with high pointed vault above. There has been another main

[47]

storey higher, and a garret, but these are now roofless. The
masonry of this part has suffered much at the hands of despoilers.

The 16th-century portion is much better preserved, its L-
planned, four-storey bulk being enhanced by two attractive stair-
towers, in addition to the aforementioned great external angle-
tower. The larger of these inward-facing towers, containing the
main stair, is corbelled out to the square at top to form the usual
16th-century watch-chamber. How the smaller tower was finished
is not now evident. Both towers have stringcourses, are pierced
by narrow slit-windows, and have doors opening on to the courtyard, with empty panel spaces above. The east wing of the L
seems to have been lower than the rest, and is now fragmentary.

Internally this portion of the castle has contained three barrel-
vaulted chambers, without fireplaces strangely, for they appear to
be living rooms, with another in the foot of the south-east tower.
On the first floor is a fine apartment, really another Hall, which
projects over the entrance pend. It has a withdrawing-room to the
east and this has access to a private room in the wing. There was
ample bedroom accommodation higher.

The great old kitchen was in one of the lean-to buildings to the
west. There is a circular well in the centre of the courtyard.

Balvenie anciently belonged to the great family of De Moravia.
The Douglases, in their spectacular rise to power, gained it. They
fell, under James the Second, but the castle was granted to John
Stewart, 2nd Earl of Atholl, whose wife was the widow of the
Earl of Douglas. The Stewarts retained it until the early 17th

century, so the 16th-century work is of their building. In 1614 it was sold by Sir James Stewart, Lord Ochiltree, to Robert Innes, 5th of Innermarkie, who was created a baronet in 1631. He and his son, staunch royalists, suffered much in the Civil War, and in 1687 Balvenie had to be sold, to Duff of Braco, ancestor of the up-and-coming Duff Earls of Fife.

Despite its strength and eminence, I have not heard of Balvenie having to withstand any major assaults.

## BLAIRFINDY CASTLE

Remotely situated in a strong position amongst the steep foothill country of Lower Glen Livet, about 5 miles due south of Ballindalloch, on Spey, Blairfindy is an interesting and substantial tower-house of the late 16th century, now ruinous but fairly intact externally to the wallhead. It is built on a variation of the favoured L-plan, with main block lying north and south, and a stair-wing projecting westwards at the south end, so placed as to form two re-entrant angles, facilitating defence. A very narrow stair-turret rises above first floor level in the main or north-west re-entrant, below which is the arched doorway. This is protected by a square shot-hole to the left, and above, at eaves-level, there is a large machicolated projection for further defence of the door. An angle-turret projected, on label-type corbelling, enhances the north-east

gable of the main block, provided with small shot-holes. The windows throughout are notably small, and the masonry is of fairly rough local rubble. Above the doorway is a heraldic panel displaying the quartered arms of Gordon, the initials I.G. and H.G. and the date 1586.

The basement is vaulted, the entrance passage giving access to the wide turnpike stair in the wing, on the right, and on the left to the large vaulted kitchen at the north end of the main block, which has a great arched fireplace, oven and stone drain. There is also a wine-cellar to the south, with the usual provision of a private stair, in the thickness of the east walling, to the Hall above. The Hall occupies all of the first floor, and has been a fine apartment, having a good fireplace on the east, and provided with a wall-chamber in the north-west angle having its own window. The turret-stair to the upper floors, now inaccessible, is narrow.

Blairfindy, built to command the important pass of Livet, from Banffshire into Aberdeenshire, also served as a hunting-seat for the Earls of Huntly. But it was originally a Grant possession, William, second son of the 10th laird of Grant being, about 1470, the progenitor of the Grants of Blairfindy. The present castle, however, appears to date substantially from the period of the heraldic panel, by which time the property had passed to the Gordons—although they may have enlarged and adapted a previous fortalice on the site. Soon after this date, in 1594, the Battle of Glenlivet was fought nearby, where its owner, the Earl of Huntly, with the Earl of Erroll and other insurgent Catholics, defeated the Protestant government army under the young Earl of Argyll, with the slaughter of over 700 of Argyll's Highlanders, allegedly for the loss of only 14 Catholic gentlemen, a short-lived triumph.

## CARNOUSIE HOUSE

This now derelict but highly attractive fortalice stands in rolling green foothill country to the north of the Deveron, four miles south-east of Aberchirder. The fabric has in recent years deteriorated badly, part of the house now being used as a piggery for the nearby farm—a sad fate for a distinguished and picturesque building.

It is a large house of the late 16th century, on the Z-plan so popular in the North-East, with main block lying east and west and towers projecting to the north-west and south-east, the former

square and gabled, the latter round with a conical roof. A stair-
turret rises in the main re-entrant, and another tiny turret-stair is
corbelled out above second-floor level in the southern re-entrant
formed by the same tower and main gable. This is to give access
to the watch-chamber in the top of the tower, which rises a storey
higher than does the rest of the house. 18th-century work has been
added to the north-east, and there have been unsightly lean-to
outbuildings erected to the south. The walls, roughcast, rise to
three storeys and a garret. The chimney-stacks, some massive,
have moulded copes. At basement level on the wall of the south-
east round tower is a water-catchment basin, with duct to carry
the water within.

The entrance is by an arched doorway in the east side of the
north tower, and gives access to a scale-and-platt stair which rises
in the tower only to the first floor, above which the ascent is continued by the turret-stair turnpike. There is a shot-hole in this
turret, at second floor level now plastered-over externally. The
basement is vaulted throughout, and the kitchen has a large arched
fireplace. The Hall, a fine room on the first floor, has a handsome
fireplace with carved overmantel showing designs of lions and
unicorns. There is still considerable good pine panelling and ornamental woodwork within.

This commodious and once-handsome mansion has passed
through many hands. Early references to the lands show them to
have been a property of the great Dunbar family, scions of the

Dunbar Earls of Moray in the 15th century. In 1530 James the Fifth granted to Walter Ogilvy of Monycabock the lands of Carnousie, resigned by James Dunbar of Cumnock. He erected them into the barony of Carnousie. In 1583, Walter Ogilvy of Carnousie sold the barony, with the 'newly constructed fortalice' to his brother, Sir George Ogilvy of Dunlugas—which dates the house. In 1622, Sir George Ogilvy, harassed by the hostile acts of neighbours petitioned the Privy Council, complaining that Robert Innes of that Ilk, Walter Innes of Auchintoul and others 'hound and chaise the cattle off the commonty of Carnousie, threaten their herds, cast faill, dovett and uther fewall on the lands, and commit uther acts of evill nycht-bourheade'. It might be mentioned that Ogilvy had been long in debt to the Inneses.

In 1639, after the celebrated Trot of Turriff, Lord Banff fell sick and was 'caried to Carnousie, where he lay a long tyme. Altho he deserted the seruice (of the King) from thencefurth, yet his cusine germane, Sir George Ogilvie of Carnousies and his brother bairnes who had been upon the seruice hithertills, could never be drawn from the royall pairtie altho they were both ruined by it.'

This ruination seemingly caused Carnousie to be sold to Sir George Gordon, eldest son of the Laird of Park nearby. In 1758 the Lady Janet Duff, widow of Sir William Gordon of Park, died at Carnousie.

## CROMBIE CASTLE

Standing above a burn two miles west of Aberchirder, Crombie is the much altered remains of a strong castle, now attached to a farmhouse, but kept in repair by Sir Thomas Innes of Learney, lately Lord Lyon. Plain and massive, and lowered as to roof-line, it now consists of an L-shaped building, with main block lying north and south and wing projecting westwards. The wing gable is surmounted by open rounds, not original and somewhat unsightly. The walls, rising from a basement plinth to crowstepped gables, are roughcast and well provided with both gunloops and shot-holes. A later and lower extension has been added to the west, in the former courtyard, linked by the simple arched entrance, and this is still occupied. The main fabric was probably built about 1543.

The door, guarded by a gunloop and machicolated projection directly above, is in the re-entrant and admits to the vaulted basement chambers, right and left, with a straight stair rising between, directly opposite the door—an unusual arrangement which is probably a reconstruction. The kitchen, to the right, has a large arched fireplace, two ovens and a water-stoup. The other vaulted chamber was the wine-cellar, with private mural stair to the Hall above. There is a small chamber off, with a pointed vault, provided with gunloop and recess. The external opening for the gun-loop is oblong, not the usual oval.

On the first floor the Hall has undergone some alteration. There is a peculiar inward projection at the north-east corner, which looks as though it should house another stairway, but does not. The turnpike stair which rises at this level is in the centre of the block, and is narrow and steep. The oval gunloop under the eastern window is interesting on account of its fluted splaying. On the next floor, the reason for the inward projection below is discoverable—but only after close examination. There is an interesting secret apartment in it, reachable only by a well-hidden trap-door; oddly enough, the fact that something is here is rather given away by two very evident spy-holes therefrom, to look down into the Hall below. Presumably arras, or other covering, was used to mask them.

The stair-head and attic storey demonstrate how the roof-level has been lowered. The building is well supplied with small re-cesses.

In 1453 there was a charter of the barony of Crombie to Sir Walter Innes, 12th of that Ilk—obtained no doubt through the

marriage of Sir Alexander, 9th laird, with the daughter of Sir David de Aberchirder, last Thane thereof. William Innes of Crombie received remission from the Privy Council for stealing goods and two oxen from Thomas Geddes in 1505. In 1547 James Innes of Crombie fell at Pinkie—so he it was who probably built this house.

There is here an interesting link with the famous Frendraught tragedy. Sir John Innes of Crombie, with Gordon of Rothiemay, were charged with letters of Treason in that they insulted William Craig, Ross Herald 'in his diplayit coat-of-arms', who had summoned them 'to have rendered and delivered the house and castle of Crommey' and to 'enter and ward at Blackness'. Instead, however, the laird threatened the herald and his assistants with their lives and vowed that 'notwithstanding His Majesty's laws, and in despite of the Lords of the Privy Council, they shall never pay the Laird of Frendraught his monies, and they shall kill him'. They accordingly besieged Crichton of Frendraught in nearby Kinnairdy Castle.

Alexander Innes of Crombie was murdered by his kinsman, Innes of Innermarkie in 1580, in barbarous circumstances, and his successor, John Innes of that Ilk, was put to the horn in 1624 for 'striking and dinging the Kirk Officer of Aberchirder'. This seems to have been the Innes swan-song, until the present Sir Thomas's time, for Crombie passed to the Urquhart family in 1631, and thereafter to the Meldrums and Duffs.

## CULLEN HOUSE

This great house, seat of the Ogilvie-Grant family, Earls of Seafield and successors of the Earls of Findlater, is not easy to describe, because of its size and the large additions and alterations which have been made to it at various periods. It stands, in a notably strong position at a bend above the deep ravine of the Burn of Deskford, south of the burgh of Cullen, and its southmost towers dizzily overhang the steep drop—although from the other side of the house the impression is of a huge modern mansion in the Scottish-Baronial style, beloved of the Victorians, as remodelled by David Bryce.

While there is probably older work incorporated, the nucleus of the present house is an L-shaped tall house of the mid-16th and early 17th centuries, which forms the angle of the two lengthy ranges of building. This was extended in 1711 and very large additions and alterations followed in 1858 and later, wholly renewing the east front. The best impression of the original forta-lice is to be gained from the courtyard to the west, where the L-planned house with its stair-wing rising a storey higher to a watch-chamber with angle-turrets, is plainly discernible. The richness of heraldic and decorative stonework, stringcourses and dormer pediments, is noteworthy. One window is particularly fine, and others enhanced with figures representing Faith, Hope and Charity, Father Time, Old Age and Youth.

The original doorway, highly ornamental, is in the usual place within the re-entrant, but this has been built up into a window and a later handsome entrance opened a little way to the north. The interior has been so greatly altered to suit later additions and requirements that no description of the original accommodation is of value. However, the usual arrangement of vaulted basement with kitchen and cellarage, Hall on first floor and bedrooms higher, would apply.

Sir Walter Ogilvie of Auchleven, younger brother of that Sir John Ogilvy who received a grant of Airlie Castle in Angus in the mid-15th century, married the heiress daughter, Margaret, of Sir John Sinclair of Deskford and Findlater, and Cullen has been

the home of their descendants since they moved from Findlater Castle nearby in the 16th century. In the seventh generation their descendent, Sir William Ogilvie, whose arms with those of his wife, Mary Douglas, dated 1603 appear on the west front, was created 1st Earl of Findlater. That title expired with the 7th Earl in 1811, when the lands passed, through the female line, to the Grant of Grant family, who inherited only the later Earldom of Seafield.

Cullen is notable for its magnificent collection of pictures, notably family portraits, many by famous masters. Interesting are those of Mary Beaton, one of 'the Queen's Maries' who married Ogilvie of Boyne, nearby; of James, 4th Earl of Findlater and 1st of Seafield, Chancellor of Scotland at the time of the Union, whose laconic remark 'There's an end to an auld sang!' is famous; and James, 6th and 3rd Earl (1714-70). This last used to suffer fits of madness, and on these occasions, when he felt the trouble coming on, used to lock himself up in the Library and drop the key out of the window to his Factor—who waited for a suitable interval and then came and released the Earl. Unhappily, one day the Factor failed to wait long enough, and opening the door was murdered by his master. So distressed was the Earl by this tragedy that his ghost allegedly used to haunt the Pink Staircase, and eventually became so troublesome that a priest was brought in to exorcise it—since when it has been seen no more.

## MAINS OF DRUMMUIR

This modest but interesting building, now a farmhouse, is set remotely, high on a hillside above the Water of Davidston close to the Aberdeenshire border, two miles south of Auchindachy Station. It was the early predecessor of the great modern Drummuir Castle which lies three miles westwards. A small, roughly-built L-shaped house of probably the early 17th century, it rises to three storeys at the front, or eastern side, but contains a storey less to the rear, owing to the steeply rising ground at that side. The architectural style is plain, but sturdy, with small windows, dormers facing the east, crowstepped gables, and a number of shot-holes. It has many similarities to Davidston House, just across the valley in Aberdeenshire, notably in the rough masonry and the manner in which the crowsteps are made up of small stones. The present forestair against the east front is modern, the original door no doubt being within the re-entrant angle. Interesting is the triple shot-hole group at first-floor level in the west wall of the main block. A dormer pediment, with the weather-worn monogram A.A.D. has been inserted in a built-up window space in the north gable. Later farm buildings have been added to the west.

Internally practically no features of interest remain. The basement cellars, provided with no fewer than five shot-holes, are not vaulted.

Alexander Leslie of Kininvie granted the lands of Drummuir to his son George, before 1549. A grandson of this George Leslie of Drummuir became the famous General Leslie, 1st Earl of Leven. William Duff, merchant in Inverness, third son of Alexander Duff of Clunybeg, was the ancestor of the Duffs of Drummuir. He died in 1715, aged 83. The same year, Alexander Duff of Drummuir, Provost of Inverness, seized the town in the Jacobite interest, and brought in his son-in-law, the Laird of Mackintosh, at the head of his clan. The Provost had earlier bought the ruined estate of Culbin, overblown with sand, for his second son John. Of this line came the first Duff Earl of Fife, and many notable Duff families in the North-East. It is perhaps of interest to note that in the subsequent Rising of 1745, Prince Charles Edward and his enemy the Duke of Cumberland successively occupied the same bed in the town-house in Church Street, Inverness, of Catherine Duff, Lady Drummuir. She used to say that 'she's lodged twa kings' bairns, but ne'er wished to lodge any more'.

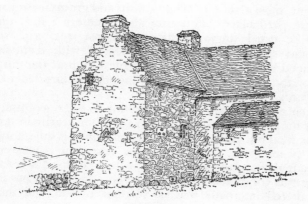

It is said that there used to be an inscription in stone at Drummuir commemorating the building of the fortalice which said ADAM DUFF AND ANNE ABERCROMBY BIGGIT THIS HOUSE AND THINK NO SHAME. This laird remarried after Anne Abercromby's death, in 1671—so the building was prior to that date. It was the daughter of this couple, who carried on the line, marrying her cousin, at the age of fifteen, Alexander Duff. A portrait is extant of this presumably plain-faced heiress, inscribed: 'Katherine Duff of Drummuir, ugly enough to be sure!'

The Duffs are still Lairds of Drummuir, although they now occupy the more modern castle, and the old house takes the name of the Mains.

## FORDYCE CASTLE

This attractive small fortalice is unusual in that it stands, not in parkland or garden but in the centre of the little village of the same name, in green braeside country three miles south-west of Portsoy, not even a wall separating its picturesquely sturdy masonry from the village street. Apart from this Fordyce is a typical L-planned laird's house of the late 16th century, with slightly later addition, two storeys and an attic in height in the main block, with the stair-wing rising a storey higher. It is notably well provided with shot-holes, has a stair-turret in the re-entrant and circular angle-turrets crowning two of the corners. For so small a place the standard of construction and masonwork is surprisingly high. The corbelling supporting the stair-turret is remarkable in that each of the eleven courses is of a different design, some most elaborate. The patterns and grouping of the shot-holes are particularly interesting also. There are four types of these—the usual single circular apertures; quatrefoil singles; triple and quadruple groups ornamented with diamond and star-shaped holes; and an unusual triple group at the north-east angle of the stair-wing at second-floor level, directed to shoot downwards.

The entrance is in the normal position in the re-entrant, at the foot of the stair-wing. The door to the right nearby in the main block is modern. Above the original doorway is an empty ornamental panel space, dated 1592. The basement is vaulted. The main stair rises, in the wing, only to the first floor, above which the ascent is continued by the turret stair. The house has been so much altered internally that no features remain, but the usual

arrangement of Hall on first floor and bedroom accommodation above applied here. A later wing was added to the east, in line with the main block.

The castle was built in 1592 by Thomas Menzies, a burgess of Aberdeen whose family had frequently held the provostship of that city. Fordyce village was formerly of greater importance than today, being erected into a burgh of barony in 1499 at the behest of the famous Bishop Elphinstone, of Aberdeen, Chancellor of Scotland. It received another charter in 1592, the year of the building of the castle.

## INCHDREWER CASTLE

High on the bare uplands three miles south-west of Banff, Inchdrewer stands out like a sentinel. When visited by the author in 1966, it was but a ruinous shell of a house, but restoration work had started on it, and it was to be built up once more into an occupiable house. By the time this appears in print, its appearance may be very different from that shown in the sketch.

Although the Inchdrewer property is very ancient, belonging in the 13th and 14th centuries to the Barclay of Towie family, passing to the Earl of Crawford in 1414, and others thereafter, the present work appears to date from no earlier than the 16th and 17th centuries. We read that Sir Walter Ogilvie of Dunlugas or his son

Sir George, bought it from the Curror family at the end of the 16th century. Both these men much added to their lands during the troubled Reformation period. Sir George, the son, also acquired Boyne nearby and built that great castle. He probably enlarged and remodelled an existing fortalice at Inchdrewer. His descendant, the first Lord Banff (created 1642) made Inchdrewer his principal residence, and in his time it was partially destroyed by General Munro, in 1640. In 1713 a tragedy occurred here, when George, Lord Banff was murdered, it was thought, by thieving domestics, who thereupon burned the building to conceal their crime. Evidently it was again rebuilt, for the house was said to be entire when the 8th and last Lord Banff died in 1803. Thereafter the property came to descendants, the Abercromby baronets of Birkenbog nearby.

Originally the building appears to have been an L-shaped tower, with the door in the re-entrant angle, above which, supported on a squinch arch, rises a slender stair-turret—to be seen to the left in the sketch. The gable with the arched doorway and the angle-turret, facing the viewer, was the wing of the L. Then, in the Ogilvie remodelling, an extension was made to the main block southwards, the new round stair-tower added, and the roof-line altered. New ranges of subsidiary building were added to the west, on the north and south sides of the courtyard; also flanking towers, traces of one of which at the south-west angle of the yard, are still to be seen, with triple-opening shot-holes.

The original stair was within the wing near the re-entrant door-

way, and gave access to the first floor only, the ascent being continued in the stair-turret. This main stair was removed when the new round tower was built, and the door removed to its present position in the west gable of the wing, facing the courtyard. The Hall was on the first floor of the main block, and this was enlarged at the rebuilding by adding the wing space to it, the dividing wall being removed. The kitchen was transferred to the south subsidiary range.

The restoration of this interesting but much-ruined house to habitable state will be a major task, but very worth-while.

## KILMAICHLIE HOUSE

Situated remotely in the picturesque wooded glen of the Avon, about four miles south of Ballindalloch, Kilmaichlie is an attractive small laird's house of apparently the early 17th century, which has seen considerable alteration and which is now a hill farmhouse. It stands high above the river in what has been quite a strong position, over a mile north of the ruined stronghold of Drumin.

The building conforms to the T-plan, an oblong main block of three storeys lying north and south, with a square stair-tower projecting in the centre of the east front and rising a storey higher, to contain a gabled watch-chamber slightly projected on simple continuous corbelling. The walls, which are fairly thick, are roughcast, and rise from a substantial basement course. There is crowstepping on only the stair-tower gables—although the roof-level of the main block may have been lowered, for there has

evidently been an angle-turret at the south-east corner of the main house, of which only the lowest corbel, in the shape of a carved head, remains.

The doorway would originally be in the foot of the tower, but this has been removed to the north, where there is a modern porch. The stair in the tower is also gone, and a modern one substituted internally. There are no internal features of interest surviving.

The lands and barony of Kilmaichlie were part of the great estates of Alexander Stewart, Earl of Buchan, fourth son of Robert the Second, the first of the Stewart kings—he who earned the soubriquet of Wolf of Badenoch. He had no legitimate offspring, and gave the lands of Strathavon, including Drumin and Kilmaichlie, to his bastard son Sir Andrew Stewart. *His* son, Sir Walter, sold the rest of Inveravon to the Gordons, but retained Kilmaichlie. It remained with his descendants until purchased by Ludovick, Laird of Grant, in the ntury, 18th cesince when it has been part of the Ballindalloch estate.

Here, late in the 18th century, the Dowager Lady Grant of Ballindalloch lived, and was visited by her godson, Henry Mackenzie, friend of Scott and author of *The Man of Feeling*. He left a charming description of the old lady and her life at Kilmaichlie, with the beauties of the situation, which has been termed 'the tenderest Scottish portrait before Sir Walter'.

In the disastrous floods of 1768, the water is said to have cut a channel through the basement of Kilmaichlie, high-set as it is.

## KININVIE HOUSE

This highly attractive fortalice, to which a later mansion has been attached, stands in pleasant wooded foothill country, in lower Glen Fiddich, three miles north of Dufftown. Although the original part of the house is said by some to have been erected about 1480, and reconstructed a century later, it in fact gives every appearance of being homogeneous, a typical L-shaped tower-house of the second half of the 16th century, with extensions of the early 18th century and later. The tall fortalice consists of a main block of four storeys and a garret, lying north and south, with a circular stair-tower projecting at the south-west corner, which rises a storey higher to end in a gabled watch-chamber corbelled out to the square. The walls, which are roughcast and whitewashed, are rounded at the angles, and pierced by arrow-slits at basement level and with comparatively small windows above. The doorway is in the re-entrant angle, guarded by a diamond-shaped shot-hole. There is a weather-worn heraldic panel in the north gable of the 18th-century building, with defaced arms, the initials W.L. and C.D. and the motto HOLD FAST. The royal arms of James the Fifth are said to appear above one of the dormer windows.

The basement is vaulted, and a good turnpike stair admits to all floors. Internally the accommodation has been adjusted to link up with the more modern house, but the Hall would be on the first floor, with sleeping accommodation above, as usual. The watch-chamber, which is known as the Charter-room, has its own fireplace. There is a circular doocot nearby.

Kininvie was a Leslie house, the patrimony of a cadet branch of the chiefly house from the early 16th century. A charter by John, 3rd Earl of Atholl to Alexander Leslie is dated 1521. This Alexander's recumbent effigy, in armour, lies in the parish church of Mortlach. He was a descendant of the 4th Baron of Balquhain, in Aberdeenshire. Having acquired the lands of Kininvie from Atholl he is said to have built the house in 1525, dying in 1549. King James the Fifth is reputed to have hidden in the kitchen of Kininvie at this period—he who was famed for his travelling in disguise, as the Gudeman of Ballengeich. As I have said, however, the general appearance of the building gives the impression of a

slightly later date than this. Alexander's eldest son Walter succeeded to Kininvie, while a younger brother got Drummuir. The eldest daughter of the 5th Leslie of Kininvie was the mother of the famous Archbishop Sharp. The 7th laird was Provost of Banff, and sold Kininvie to his third brother, John, in 1703—who in 1726 built the middle section of the house, dying in 1732. The house is still occupied and in excellent condition.

## KINNAIRDY CASTLE

Situated in a very strong position high above a ravine, two miles south of Aberchirder, Kinnairdy is a most interesting and picturesque building, somewhat altered as to its upper storeys, once the chief fortalice of the ancient thanage and barony of Aberchirder.

The castle is now L-shaped, but the stair-tower is of later date, and the original appears to have been an oblong keep of five storeys, with parapet and walk, dating from the mid-15th century. In the early 18th century the upper storeys were altered and the castle reroofed, with crowstepped gables. It has been discovered that the crowsteps were formed out of the corbels of the original parapet. The stair-tower is surmounted by a small gabled watch-chamber, very similar to that at Durris in Kincardineshire. The castle was formerly strengthened by a curtain-wall with gatehouse.

The original entrance was at first-floor level, probably reached from the courtyard-wall parapet-walk by a removable timber bridge. A straight stair led down to the vaulted basement. This is now reachable from the lower extension to the east, and has a notably high vault, with ceiling opening. There is a garderobe in the north wall. The Hall above has three deep window-embrasures, enlarged. In the north wall is the celebrated oak-panelled aumbry, with carving reputed to be the finest in Scotland, dating from 1493, bearing the carved heads of Sir Alexander Innes, 13th of that Ilk, and his wife Dame Christian Dunbar. There is a large fireplace, removed from where the aumbry is now. The second floor is now subdivided, and has stone window-seats and a small moulded fireplace. There is much excellent heraldic decoration about the house, some of it introduced by the present owner, Sir Thomas Innes of Learney, lately Lord Lyon.

Sir Alexander Innes, 9th of that Ilk, married the heiress of Sir David de Aberchirder, last Thane thereof. Sir James Innes, 12th, settled his son Alexander in Kinnairdy in 1487. This Sir Alexander

was extravagant, for instance importing much carved work from Flanders—as witness the aumbry-panelling above mentioned. Eventually, because of his unpaid debts, his relatives petitioned for him to be handed over to one of them, the Earl of Caithness, and he was shut up in Girnigoe Castle as 'ane misguided man and prodigious, and has wastit and destroyit his lands and guids without ony reasonable occasion'. He died in 1537, and his son, Alexander, 14th, had to grant a life-rent of Kinnairdy to his father-in-law, Lord Forbes.

Sir Robert, the 20th, sold Kinnairdy to Sir James Crichton of Frendraught, the laird involved in the celebrated tragedy of 1629. As described under Crombie Castle, Sir John Innes and Gordon of Rothiemay attempted to attack Crichton in Kinnairdy, but the place was too strong for them. 'They came by way of hamesucken to the complainer's house of Kinnairdy, . . . fished in his waters nearby, and rade up and doon beside the place in a bragging manner and used all manner of provocation to have drawn furth the complainer to have slain him.' Out of this resulted the eventual grim burning of the Tower of Frendraught.

In 1647 the Rev. John Gregory, minister of Drumoak, got a grant of Kinnairdy. His brother David succeeded. This was the famous medical man and inventor. The first barometer in Scotland was made by him here. He was otherwise accomplished, having 29 children, and died aged 95 in 1720. His third son, Professor David Gregory, of Oxford, sold Kinnairdy to Thomas Donaldson, merchant in Elgin. He it was who restored and remodelled the castle.

## MAINS OF MAYEN

Here is an interesting and attractive small laird's house, apparently of the first half of the 17th century, and extended later in the same century, situated on a commanding and slant-wise site above the green Deveron valley two miles east of Rothiemay. Although now called The Mains, it was the original mansion of this ancient property.

The house conforms to the L-plan, with a circular stair-tower in the re-entrant angle, the harled walls rising, from a massive boulder-and-outcrop foundation course, two storeys to crowstepped gables, a steep roof of stone slates, and dormer windows. The main block lies approximately east and west, with the wing extending southwards. This wing, however, is clearly of later date. The stair-tower, larger than usual and with peculiar little dormer windows of its own, also appears to belong to the later period, although it almost certainly replaces an earlier and smaller turnpike in the same position.

The present doorway lies in the north front, though the original probably would be in the foot of the stair-tower. It is moulded and square-headed, and over it is a delightfully coloured heraldic panel dated 1680, bearing the arms of Abernethy and Hacket, or Halkett with the initials A.A. and I.H. A dormer nearby is also dated 1680, the period of the enlargement. The basement is not vaulted, and the interior has obviously been considerably altered in the late 17th century, and undergone restoration in modern times. The main block now contains three apartments intercommunicating, the central one having much character, with a very large fireplace provided with salt-box and an aumbry nearby. In the thick north wall of the western room is a garderobe with its own tiny window. This chamber has a moulded stone fireplace in the gable. The upper floor has been modernised.

The history of Mayen is of great interest. The property originally was part of the barony of Rothiemay which David Second bestowed on his faithful adherent William de Abernethy, in the 14th century. In 1445 the then Abernethy laird became the first Lord Saltoun. The family held the property until 1612, when it passed to the Gordons. However, Mayen at least came back to

[66]

the Abernethys. In 1649 Walter Hacket, in Milltown of Rothiemay, Sheriff-Clerk of Banff, purchased Mayen, and dying seven years later, his daughter and co-heiress Isobel carried it to her husband Alexander Abernethy, a cadet of Saltoun, in 1665. It is this couple's arms and initials which grace the north front, and who obviously were responsible for the alterations and extensions. They were involved in an extraordinary situation. In 1612 the 8th Lord Saltoun disponed most of his estates, and died in 1617 leaving a son of only six. When this 9th Lord came of age, he repudiated his father's alienations of the estate, amidst a mass of litigation. The Clerk of Session of the period happened to be James Abernethy, brother of Alexander, laird of Mayen, and when the Scots public records were being removed to London, he was in a position secretly to tear out the three relevant pages of the court proceedings, secreting them in the walling of Mayen House. With his kinsman, the 9th Lord, he then contested the disponing at law, and there being no documentary evidence now available for the defence, the case was won and the alienations declared invalid. The vital papers remained hidden in the wall. James Abernethy predeceased his brother, and when the laird was dying, in 1683, he left the secret with his kinsman James Ogilvie, who with the lady of the house made a stealthy candlelight search one night, when all the family were asleep, and found the three pages behind the laird's own built-in bed. The secret weighed heavily on Ogilvie's mind, and on his own deathbed in 1691 he made declaration of it. A year later the papers were produced in court and the earlier judgement reversed.

[67]

The Abernethys of this line, however, remained at Mayen. John, Alexander's successor, was one of the Jacobite lairds who surrendered at Banff in 1715. James, *his* son, shot dead John Leith of Leith Hall, after an election meeting, in an Aberdeen street, and escaping abroad, was outlawed. Fortunately his wife came of the rich and powerful family of Duff, and they came to the rescue. James the 4th laird died unmarried and intestate in 1785, and Major Alexander Duff, cousin, and husband of his elder sister, bought Mayen. He it was who in 1788 started to build the more modern mansion nearby.

## PARK HOUSE

The ancient fortalice of the Gordons of Park is not at first easily discernible in the midst of the large mansion which has been added to it at various periods; but a little examination, outside and in, establishes it as a tall Z-planned tower-house of a type quite common in the North-East, more or less embedded in the south end of the building. The house stands within a large estate in the parish of Ordiquhill about seven miles south of Portsoy.

The nucleus would appear to date from the second half of the 16th century, and consists of a main block lying north and south, with towers or wings projecting to the north-east and south-west. It is the latter portion which is shown in sketch, the former being hidden within the later work. The actual south-west gable appears to date from the early 18th century, when there was the main enlargement to the fortalice, but the re-entrant angle is original, and contains the early arched and moulded entrance doorway, now reduced to the status of window. Above, at second floor-level, is a very fine heraldic panel, somewhat weatherworn but apparently displaying the arms of Gordon. Within the re-entrant rises a slender stair-tower, unusual in that, almost like a turret, it is corbelled out somewhat at first-floor level. The narrow turnpike stair however rises within the lower portion from ground level, just to the right of the entrance. The walling is harled over, so that it is very difficult to trace the exact limits of the earlier work.

A range of vaulted cellars occupies the basement, as usual. At the north-east end rises another narrow turnpike stair. The normal arrangement of Hall on first floor and bedroom accommodation above, would apply.

The large semi-circular towers, dating from the early 18th century, have been superimposed on the west front and south gable

[68]

of the main block. At the foot of the latter is a handsome moulded doorway with an inscribed lintel, weatherworn, but on which can still be discerned the name Elphinstone and the date 1723.

The Gordons of Park took an active part in the affairs of the North-East. The lairds thereof now bracket the name of Duff with Gordon, and the Park family seem to have had links with the Duffs over a long period. In the early 18th century, for instance, Helen Gordon, daughter of Sir James, of Park, married John, second son of Duff of Drummuir, who gave the young people the famous estate of Culbin, overblown with sand in 1705—which, in typical Duff fashion he had no doubt bought at a bargain price. Then, in the Rising of 1745, Sir William Gordon of Park took the side of Prince Charles Edward, was attainted, but escaping overseas, died at Douay in France in 1751. He was married, apparently just before this transpired, to the Lady Jane Duff, a daughter of the first Earl of Fife—which certainly must have upset the cautious and acquisitive Duffs. Nevertheless, attainder or none, the family is still at Park.

# BUTE

## ASCOG HOUSE

Situated within the grounds of a more modern mansion, about two miles south-east of Rothesay, Ascog is a tall old house of the early 17th century, now divided into flats. The building has been much altered and added to, both in the late 17th century and later; but it appears to have been originally an L-shaped structure of main block of two storeys and an attic, lying north and south, with a stair-tower projecting eastwards and rising a storey higher to end in a gabled watch-chamber slightly projected on corbelling. The gables are crowstepped, the roofs steep, the chimneys coped and the masonry of a pinkish coursed rubble. The watch-chamber has its own fireplace and chimney-stack.

The floor levels have been altered, obviously, as the position of walled-up windows reveals. An unusual projection is corbelled out on the north face of the stair-tower at watch-chamber level, for purposes unknown. Below is an empty heraldic panel-space. Another such panel-space decorates the walling on the west side of the main block; and there is a broken inscribed stone, now indecipherable, built into the east face of the stair-tower. One of the altered dormers of the east front is dated 1678.

The entrance is now by a modern wooden porch within the south re-entrant angle, with the fairly wide stair rising to the right. With the changed floor-levels, the interior of the house has been so altered as to retain no original features.

Ascog, during the period of this building, was the property of a Stewart family, stemming from that of Kilchattan, this itself being a cadet branch of the Stewarts of Bute. The first of Ascog seems to have been second son of that Kilchattan who married a daughter of Fairlie of that Ilk in 1584. His son, John Stewart of Ascog, married a daughter of Kelso of Kelsoland in Ayrshire, and he was succeeded by Ninian, served heir of his father in 1637.

Their chief, Sir John Stewart of Bute, having suffered greatly for supporting Charles the First, petitioned Charles the Second for aid in rebuilding Rothesay Castle, much damaged by Cromwell, but like so many others, was disappointed. Ninian Stewart of Ascog advanced large sums to aid him. Because of the date 1678 on the dormer above-mentioned, it has been assumed that this house was built by the next laird, John; but obviously the original building is older than this. In 1704 a John Stewart of Ascog was a Commissioner of Supply. In the mid-18th century Ascog passed by marriage of the heiress, to Murray of Blackbarony, in Peebles-shire, and thereafter to a more distant relative, Archibald Mac-Arthur of Milton, who adopted the name of Stewart, an Edin-burgh celebrity immortalised in *Kay's Portraits*, being exceedingly mean and eccentric enough to keep pigs in his bedroom. An Archibald Stewart of Ascog, whether this or a successor, in 1813 bore part of the cost of building a road from Rothesay.

## BRODICK CASTLE, ARRAN

This well-known ducal seat, now the property of the National Trust for Scotland, though largely modern, incorporates an ancient castle, famous in history, at its east end. The site is a strong one, with the ground dropping away sharply to east and south, about a mile north of Brodick village, within a large estate. At first sight it is a little difficult to distinguish the old from the new as the additions have been built in the same style of architecture; but in fact the join, centrally along the main south front, is quite clear, with the larger windows at first-floor level as guide. The ancient parts consist of a long main block lying east and west, of three storeys and an attic, surmounted by a crenellated parapet and walk projected on three courses of continuous corbelling; plus an unusual cluster of two stair-towers linked, and a slightly taller and gabled square tower projecting northwards. Added to this is a low battery for cannon, erected by Cromwell's troops and extending eastwards. The first of the stair-towers is circular at base but corbelled out to the square above second-floor level, and the parapet continues around this tower, the head of which is a cap-house. Most of the building thus described belongs basically to the 16th and 17th centuries, but much considerably older work is incorporated in the lower storeys, dating from before Bruce's time. Some of the windows, which are regularly placed, have been enlarged. One or two early wide splayed gunloops remain. The masonry is an excellent warm red coursed rubble.

The original entrance was to the east, beside Cromwell's battery, now reached by stone steps, but formerly probably by a removable timber access. The basement chambers are vaulted, containing an old kitchen and range of cellars and pits. Some of the internal doorways have pointed-arched heads. Turnpike stairs rise in the two linked towers, an unusual arrangement. Higher, the accommodation has been much altered and modernised. 'Bruce's Room' is still pointed out.

[73]

Brodick's story is a long and exciting one and can only be hinted at here. It was allegedly first a Viking fort, later taken over by the Lords of the Isles. Angus of the Isles aided Bruce at the lowest ebb of his fortunes, and their men seized Brodick from the English invaders in 1307; and here the hero-king is alleged to have awaited the fire signal from his own castle of Turnberry across the Firth, for his return to the mainland. This is obviously incorrect, however; geography prevents Turnberry area from being visible from here. Moreover Brodick was much too strongly held by the English to be accessible to Bruce in 1307. The account refers to the smaller and now ruinous castle of Kildonan, at the very south tip of Arran. Passing to the Stewarts, the castle was twice sacked by the English in the succeeding century, though in 1386 it was still described as 'ane stith castell of stane'. Brodick thereafter passed into the hands of the up-and-coming Boyd family, Thomas, Lord Boyd receiving it as part of the dowry of the Princess Mary, James the Third's sister, when he became Earl of Arran. The Boyds quickly fell, and James, Lord Hamilton, marrying the widow, obtained Arran and Brodick and was in turn created Earl of Arran. The castle was burned in 1528, in feuding with the Campbells and Macleans; and again by the Earl of Lennox. In 1652 Cromwell's troops occupied Arran and built the battery. They were later surprised by Arran near Sannox, and slain to a man.

## LITTLE CUMBRAE CASTLE

Although readily seen from the steamer to Arran from Fairlie, this castle is less than easy to visit, being sited on an islet off the east side of the island of Little Cumbrae in the Firth of Clyde. It is a simple square keep of probably early 15th-century date, long ruinous but in a fair state of preservation. Three main storeys rise to the parapet and walk, which is projected on excellent chequered corbelling and has open rounds at the three angles other than that to the south-west where the stairway has risen to end in a caphouse. Above was the usual garret chamber within the gabled roof. Most of the original windows are small, and there are wide splayed gunloops at basement level, with arrow slits.

The entrance is at first-floor level, now reached by a stone forestair but formerly by a removable timber ladder, for security. A later doorway was opened into the basement, but originally the only access to the two vaulted intercommunicating ground-floor

cellars was from the first floor. Here was the Hall, also vaulted, with its own fireplace; but a large kitchen fireplace also, screened off at the west end, an early feature for a tower of this period. The turnpike stair continues to the second floor, the two chambers of which are reached by a mural passage to the south, each having a fireplace and a garderobe with seat in the north wall. The garret floor is roofless. The castle was once surrounded by a rampart and ditch.

The history of Little Cumbrae and its castle is interesting. It was apparently a royal property from very early times, possibly coming with the High Steward; and the Hunters of nearby Hunterston were hereditary keepers. There was a serious dispute in the 15th century between the Crown and the keeper over the falcons bred on the Red Farland head, which the King claimed as royal birds. The Governor of Dumbarton Castle was commanded to apprehend the Laird of Hunterston, but Hunter and his men successfully defended themselves in their remote stronghold. They remained custodians until 1515 when Hugh, Earl of Eglinton, keeper of Rothesay Castle, was appointed 'fiar, correkar and supplear of the isle of Littill Comeray, to resist and punish those destroying the wild bestis and grund of the samen quhil the King's [James the Fifth] perfite age of fifteen years, because Robert Huntare of Hunterstone, forester of heritage of the said isle, may nocht resist because he is nocht of substance and power'. The said Robert was only a boy, his father having been slain at Flodden two years before, with the King's father. However, Robert Hunter later married the daughter of Eglinton and so got back his isle. But not for long, for it was sold back to Eglinton in 1535. It seems likely therefore that it was the Earl who built the present

[75]

castle. During Cromwell's occupation, the 6th Earl roosted secure here, sufficiently to confine Cromwell's friend Archibald Hamilton herein and send him to be hanged at Stirling; whereupon in 1653, Cromwell's troops made a dead set at Cumbrae, surprising and burning it. Since when it has remained semi-ruinous.

## KAMES CASTLE

Standing within its estate on the shores of Kames Bay—the name is a corruption of *Camus*, Gaelic for bay—this is a tall and massive keep of the 14th century, formerly surrounded by a moat, traces of which still remain. Later and lower buildings are attached but do not obstruct. The keep rises four storeys to a crenellated parapet projected on simple individual corbels and drained by the usual cannon-like spouts: and within the parapet-walk is a gabled garret storey. The windows where original are very small and infrequent, but two large lights have been opened at first-floor level to the west. The masonry is coursed rubble and the walls reach approximately 6 feet in thickness, the overall measurements being 36 by 26 feet.

The entrance is by a round-headed doorway at ground level to the north, admitting to the vaulted basement. A straight and narrow stair rises within the thickness of the walling and ends in a caphouse at the north-east corner of the parapet-walk The usual arrangement of Hall on first floor and sleeping accommodation

above prevails. The building is in good order and has been somewhat restored.

This was the seat of the ancient family of Bannatyne, said to come from Ayrshire. The line appears to descend from one Gilbert, flourishing in the reign of Alexander the Third. His son Gilbert and grandson John had charters of Kames from Walter the High Steward (Bruce's son-in-law) to one of which King Robert himself was witness, in 1318. Yet in 1334 John son of Gilbert appears as Captain of nearby Rothesay Castle for Edward Baliol. The family sent four sons to Flodden. There were no fewer than eleven Bannatyne lairdships, but Kames was the principal. In 1594 Dean Munro says, after mentioning the round castle of 'Rosay': 'That uther castle callit the castle of Kames quhilk Kames in Erishe is alsmeikle as to say in English the bay castle. . . .' In 1617-39 Hector Bannatyne of Kames was a member of the Scots Parliament, and in 1704 another Hector was Commissioner of Supply for Buteshire. The last of the direct line was James, who died unmarried in 1786 aged 89. He was succeeded by his nephew, William Macleod, who took the name of Bannatyne. He was an advocate and was duly promoted to the Bench with the title of Lord Kames in 1799, and knighted. He was an original member of the antiquarian Bannatyne Club and died aged 91 in 1833. Unfortunately he lost his fortune and had to sell Kames in 1812 to James Hamilton W.S. John Sterling the critic and essayist was born at Kames, and Carlyle in his biography refers to the castle as 'a kind of delapidated baronial residence to which a small farm was then attached'. The castle is now part of a holiday centre of the Scottish Council for the Care of Spastics.

## WESTER KAMES CASTLE

This small late 16th-century fortalice, measuring only 25 by 21 feet, was long a ruin but has undergone a major restoration, so that most of the upper works are in fact modern. But the work has been very well done, and probably fairly represents the original appearance. It stands on the Island of Bute, less than a mile north of Port Bannatyne and within the estate of the larger Kames Castle, although originally it was an entirely independent lairdship. The position is not an obviously strong one.

The building is oblong, with a circular stair-tower projecting to the north-west. The walls are of good coursed rubble and rise to four storeys. The tower extends a storey higher, where it is

[77]

corbelled out to the square to form a gabled watch-chamber reached by a turret stair projecting in the south-west re-entrant. A circular angle-turret crowns the south-east corner of the building. The windows, where original, have simple roll-mouldings and are small. There are a number of shot-holes.

The entrance is by an elaborately decorative doorway in the east front, near the stair-foot. The basement is vaulted and contains two chambers, originally no doubt kitchen and wine-cellar. The main turnpike rises only to the first floor, where would be the Hall. Above this the ascent is continued by the stair in the turret. Having so long been ruinous, the interior is necessarily modernised.

At the time of Bruce, the lands now known as Wester Kames belonged to a family of MacKinlays, the laird having three sons, expert archers. After an archery contest with members of the King's entourage at Rothesay Castle nearby, at which the King's men lost, the winning MacKinlays were raided by the bad losers, and no fewer than seventeen of them were slain by the sons' accurate bowmanship. This was too much for Bruce, and the MacKinlays were sent packing, fleeing to Perthshire. The King thereafter gave the property to his butler, or dispenser or Spenser, a MacDonald, whose descendants took the name of Spens, and called their lairdship the House of Spens. They retained possession until 1670, when the little castle passed by marriage to Grahams, coming later, like most of the island, to the Bute family. The Spens lairds were prominent in the life of the community during these three and a half centuries, and Bute records abound with their activities. In 1447 Finlay de Spens was Constable of Bute.

## LOCHRANZA CASTLE, ARRAN

Dramatically sited on a small peninsula jutting into Loch Ranza at the north end of Arran, this fine castle is said to have been built originally by the Stewart kings as a hunting seat; but its strategic position is obvious. Fordun mentions it in 1400 as one of two royal castles on Arran; and Dean Munro of the Isles writes, in 1594, 'Herein are thre castils—ane callit Braizay [Brodick] pertaining to the Earl of Arran; ane uther auld hoose callit the castil of the heid of Lochrenesay, pertaining likewise to the said Earle. . . .' If it was an old house in 1594, and extant in 1400, there must be much older work incorporated than is the general impression today, which is of 16th-century construction.

The building, now ruinous, belongs to the L-plan, with the main block lying north and south and a square wing or tower projecting westwards at the south end. In the main the castle is three storeys and an attic in height, but the south tower rises two storeys higher, as did the north-east corner, which was built up into another tower, in unusual fashion, and is now very fragmentary. There is a circular angle-turret at the north-west corner, at third-floor level, and a corbelled machicolation to protect the door beneath, also at this level, nearby.

The top of the south-west tower is vaulted to support a platform roof, and there has been a caphouse to the east at the stairhead. The walls are of good coursed rubble, with pinkish freestone dressings, the windows are small and shot-holes are provided. The entrance, in the west front, is closed by an iron yett, and above is an empty heraldic panel-space. To the left, within, rises the main turnpike stair to all floors. The basement contains two vaulted chambers to the north, connected by a doorway only 4 feet high. To the right, or south, is a large unvaulted apartment, now open to the sky, with a small vaulted room off in the wing, which appears to have been the pit or prison. An angled straight stair rises in the south-east corner, now built up. A passage was screened off at this south end to give access to these. The Hall on

the first floor has a 2-foot high dais at the south end and, strangely, no fireplace—although one may have been built up. A partition wall divides off the kitchen at the north end, with a service hatch between. There is a large kitchen fireplace to the east, with its own drain and window. The upper floors were reached by the main staircase and by another turnpike in the thickness of the south wall. There was another large room above the Hall and a smaller over the kitchen and in the wing. Both towers contained watch-chambers.

The castle, from royal ownership, was granted by James the Second to Alexander, 1st Lord Montgomerie. He was succeeded by his grandson Hugh, who was keeper of both Brodick and Rothesay Castles. James the Fourth raised him to the dignity of Earl of Eglinton. In 1614 the castle was made the base for an assault, by James the Sixth's forces, on the Clan Donald federation of the Isles; and later that century was occupied by Cromwell's troops. In 1705 the property was sold by the Montgomeries to Anne, Duchess of Hamilton for £43,200 Scots.

# ROTHESAY MANSIONHOUSE

It has not been my policy to include town-houses in this survey —that is houses built as the town lodgings of lords and lairds, rather than former fortalices round which towns and cities have grown. This because such were not normally intended as defensive buildings. But in this case, while the Mansionhouse is and always has been part of a Rothesay street, it was in fact the seat of

the Stewarts of Rothesay from 1685, when the castle nearby was
burned and made uninhabitable, until the first Mountstuart House
was built; and therefore it was no mere town-house. Moreover,
it is a typical example of a class of building so frequently described
in these volumes, almost identical with Ascog House a couple of
miles away. It even has a shot-hole in its stair-tower.

Facing across to the castle, it is a substantial building of the
early 17th century, with steep roofs and crowstepped gables, consisting of a main block of three storeys, with a stair-tower projecting centrally, this being corbelled out to end in a gabled
watch-chamber rising a storey higher and having its own moulded
fireplace and chimney. It is possible that originally the house consisted of only the eastern part of the main block and the stair-
tower, forming an L, and that the western part is an extension;
for the windows of that wing are notably more regularly placed
and frequent. The walls are roughcast, so that the masonry and
any bonding is hidden. Over the doorway, which is in the eastern
re-entrant angle, is a heraldic panel, handsomely coloured, bearing
the Bute arms.

The basement is not vaulted. The building contains much good
panelling. It is now used as the Bute Estate Office. The usual
arrangement of rooms would apply.

The original house is said to have been erected by a Paisley
merchant turned laird, in the early 17th century, and the eastern
end and stair-tower appear to date from that period. Another
account declares that the house was built in 1681 by one George
Cunningham W.S.—this date appearing on a gable. If so, the
builder must have occupied his house for only a very short period
for it was in 1685 that the Earl of Argyll attacked Rothesay Castle

and rendered it uninhabitable, whereupon Sir James Stewart thereof, or Stuart as the family now spell it, purchased the Mansionhouse to dwell in. He was created 1st Earl of Bute in 1703. It is recounted that when his son, James, 2nd Earl, who married Lady Ann, daughter of Archibald 1st Duke of Argyll, brought his bride to this house, she exclaimed at its smallness; whereupon the bridegroom pointed to the ruined castle across the street saying, 'There was our house before your family burned it'! It was the son of this couple who became 3rd Earl and Prime Minister —a scarcely notable one. He also married a Campbell bride, his cousin—perhaps insurance against further Campbell inroads.

## ROTHESAY CASTLE

This famous castle is highly unusual in its circular planning, both the main wall of enceinte and the flanking towers being round, and only the gatehouse-tower oblong. It stands, however, within a square moated area, on a rock, in the centre of the town of Rothesay, and though long ruinous its main features survive and are now maintained in good condition. There has been a considerable castle here from very early times, built to resist the encroachments of the Norsemen. Whether the original castle was that built by Alan, the High Steward, in 1204, is not certain; but that building *was* captured by the Norsemen and not recovered until after the Battle of Largs in 1263.

The massive 13th-century walls are 8-10 feet thick, 20 feet high, and the diameter of the circular enclosure 142 feet. The gatehouse-tower, largely of later date but incorporating parts of the original, projects to the north and was formerly reached from a drawbridge over the moat; it is still the entrance though the bridge is now permanent. Of the four round flanking towers that to the north-west is the only one in good condition; but portions of all survive, each having a pronounced batter at the foundations, and each entered by a door from the courtyard at ground level. Of the former subsidiary buildings within the courtyard only the chapel remains, to the east, oblong, with a stairway reaching up to the wall-walk that topped the circular ramparts. This curtain-wall has been heightened at some time, and it is not certain whether the walk was within the usual stone parapet, and open, or projected within a timber hoarding. Other secondary buildings indicated now only by foundations, have been scattered about the yard.

[82]

The gatehouse keep is the most entire and interesting, although most altered feature, having been repaired and redesigned in 1520 at a cost of £191 7s. It is L-shaped and four storeys and an attic in height. Its main block terminates in a parapet projected on simple individual corbels, and has lost its garret chamber; but the wing retains its 16th-century crowstepped gable and chimney-stack though the roofing has gone. There are shot-holes in the masonry at this level. The keep, entered from the bridge, is pierced by a wide vaulted pend, and the doorway is grooved for a portcullis. A small guardroom opens off the pend to the east, and there is also a straight stair in the thickness of this wall. The Hall on the first floor measures 49 by 25 feet and has a large fire-place to the west and windows on three sides. The south end was partitioned off to form a private room, 12 feet wide, with windows overlooking the courtyard. In the projecting wing to the west were latrines with chutes down to the moat—an unusual pro-vision. The floors above are now inaccessible but there is ribbed vaulting, probably representing an oratory.

The history of Rothesay Castle is stirring, inevitably. It was of course a royal fortress and palace and the favourite seat of Robert the Second and Robert the Third, giving its name to the dukedom of the heir to the Scots throne—as it still does. It passed to Sir John Stewart the Black, illegitimate son of Robert the Second, the first Stewart king, and remained with his descendants, the Stewarts, or Stuarts, of Bute, now Marquesses of Bute. In 1685 it was attacked and burned by Argyll, and the family removed to the Mansionhouse nearby.

# CAITHNESS

## ACKERGILL TOWER

A massive and fairly simple 15th-century keep, still occupied and in good order, Ackergill stands on the rocky edge of the Caithness coast, in a less notably strong position than some of its neighbours, less than three miles north of Wick and a couple of miles west of Castle Girnigoe. Unlike so many Caithness castles, this was never a Sinclair stronghold, although obviously that warlike family coveted it. Formerly surrounded by a moat 12 feet wide by 12 feet deep, it consists of a large, plain oblong tower 65 feet in height, with walls 10 feet in thickness, rising to five storeys, the upper of which has been renewed in the 19th century, so that the gabled garret storey and the parapet and walk, open rounds and square pyramidal-roofed caphouse, are all modern, as are the out-

buildings to east, west and north. However, it is probable that the original roofline of the castle was very much as now appears. The parapet rises flush and is not projected on corbelling, and is drained by the usual spouts. Many of the windows have been enlarged.

The entrance is by an arched doorway in the south front, admitting to a passage in the wall from which a straight mural stair rises to the right to the vaulted Hall on the first floor. The basement is also vaulted. Thereafter the ascent is by a circular turnpike, diagonally across the Hall, in the north-west angle, ending at parapet-level in the aforementioned caphouse. The Hall measures 28 by 18 feet, and its vault is 23 feet high. There is a long passage in the east wall from which a small stair leads up to a minstrels' gallery half-way up the vault. The second floor contains two chambers, reached by a mural passage to the north. These are supplied with deep mural garderobes. The fourth floor is similar, and the top, of course, is modern.

Rather unusual are the twin lean-to type doocots a short distance to the south-east.

In the 13th century, Ackergill was a possession of the powerful Norman family of Cheyne, but this line failed in an heiress who in 1350 married John Keith, son of the Marischal. It remained a Keith stronghold for two centuries—although only just. In 1518 Keith of Ackergill and his son were ambushed and slain, on the way home from Inverness, by a party of Gunns for 'ancient wrong'. In 1547 Mary of Guise, the Queen-Regent, granted a remission to George, Earl of Caithness, for 'treasonable taking of Alexander Keith, Captain of Ackergill, and detaining him in Girnigoe and other places'. Again in 1556, the same Earl got another remission for beseiging the house of Ackergill belonging to the Earl Marischal. Somehow, the Lord Oliphant got a grant of the property from Mary Queen of Scots, and later it passed to the Dunbars of Hempriggs, with whom it still remains.


# BRIMS CASTLE

Remotely situated at the end of a long farm road, at the east side of the low Pentland Firth promontory of Brims Ness, five miles west of Thurso, this is a small, and simple fortalice with one or two unusual features, now unfortunately somewhat sadly neglected, though still part occupied in connection with the adjoining farm. It is a late 16th-century tower-house on the L-plan, con-

sisting of a gabled main block lying east and west, with a square stair-wing extending northwards at the east end, the roof of which has been altered, and which would no doubt originally contain the usual watch-chamber. A semi-circular open turret projects at the wallhead near the centre of the east front, to protect the access, the corbelling being chequered more elaborately than might be expected. There is a courtyard to the north, and while this has been largely filled up by later subsidiary building on the east, on the west the high curtain walling remains, with a high round-headed arched and moulded gateway facing west, over which is an empty heraldic panel space. The tower rises to three storeys and a garret, and the original windows have been small and scanty. The masonry is of the local small and flat grey Caithness rubble. The gables are crowstepped.

The doorway was at first-floor level in the wing, no doubt reached by the usual removable timber stairway, for security. There is now a modern forestair from the south. The Hall occupied this floor, and in the south-east angle a small private stair led down to the vaulted basement. There was also a hatchway in the Hall floor, through this vault. It seems that there was no external access to the ground floor chamber, though there is now a modern door. The two upper floors would provide sleeping accommodation on no very extensive scale, though there would be additional lean-to quarters within the courtyard.

The Sinclairs of Brims were cadets of Dunbeath, who themselves sprang from the House of Mey and the Earls of Caithness.

[87]

# DUNBEATH CASTLE

Situated in a typically striking cliff-top position 12 miles north of Helmsdale, and facing north across Dunbeath Bay, this handsome 17th-century house is one of the few similarly-sited Caithness castles to remain occupied and entire. Occupying the usual promontory crest and defended to landward by a deep dry ditch, it might look to be impregnable—but in fact proved otherwise on at least two occasions. The aspect and plan of the old part are both somewhat unusual. There are large modern additions to north and east.

The plan is an oblong, of four storeys, with two-storey angle-turrets enhancing all angles save that to the north-east. In the centre of the main west front two stair-turrets are corbelled out at first-floor level, and rise three storeys to terminate in small gabled watch-chambers. These, in turn, are reached by tiny turret stairs, projecting further, in the outer re-entrant angles—a picturesque elaboration. The northern of these two turrets is in fact modern, although a good copy, and replaces a similar one shown in a drawing of 1821 but missing by MacGibbon & Ross's time. The walls, reaching five feet in thickness, are harled and whitewashed, the roofs steep, the gables crowstepped, and there are numerous gunloops and shot-holes, a notable series of triple holes defending the ground floor. The round-headed doorway between the two frontal turrets is modern.

Internally there has been much alteration. The basement consists of four vaulted apartments, that in the centre being used as entrance hall. To the left is the old kitchen, with a large arched fireplace in the north gable. To the south are two inter-communicating cellars, the first of which, having a private stair in the thickness of the east wall to the Hall above, was doubtless the laird's wine-cellar. There is another tiny, and secret, stairway in the thickness of the back wall of the entrance vault, only 15 inches wide. Above has been modernised, but the turnpike stair in the southern of the frontal turrets led up from the Hall to the sleeping accommodation on the two upper floors.

The building, although it is said to contain 15th-century work, dates substantially from the first half of the 17th century. In 1452, Sir George Crichton, Lord High Admiral of Scotland, of the family which was then ruling the land, heired Dunbeath from his mother, and was created Earl of Caithness, a Sinclair title, by the young James the Second. He held neither Dunbeath nor the earldom long, for the Crichtons fell almost as quickly as they rose.

[88]

By 1507 Dunbeath was in Innes hands, but from them passed to Alexander Sinclair, son of William 2nd Sinclair Earl of Caithness, and Elizabeth Innes his wife, in 1529. In 1624 John Sinclair of Geanies, second son of Sinclair of Mey, who had made a fortune as a merchant, bought the property, and by him the present work was mainly erected. This family attained the dignity of a baronetcy in 1704. In 1648 Sir John Sinclair of Dunbeath, Knight, was a member of the Scots Parliament. In 1650 the castle was besieged by General Hurry, for Montrose, and capitulated after a few days. Later, after Montrose's defeat at Carbisdale, the Royalist garrison in turn surrendered, the water supply failing.

## FRESWICK HOUSE

Set above a sandy inlet of the cliff-bound coast about five miles south of Duncansby Head, Freswick commands one of the few landing-places of a precipitous seaboard. The site has always been recognised as a vital one, and in the Orkneyinga Saga we read of a Viking settlement here, and of the Jarl Havard of Freswick killed at a battle here in 980. Later, Sweyn Aslief is reported as looking after Freswick for his stepsons, in 1153. There are the remains of a broch nearby, and nearer still to the present house, the broken ruins of a 12th-century castle, originally also called Freswick but later named Buchollie after the property of that name in Aber-

deenshire. The House of Freswick is a very tall and towerlike
building, probably of the early 17th century, added to by a wing
of similar height probably about a century later. Standing impressively on a knoll where the small river almost forms an island
on entering Freswick Bay, it makes a notable landmark, giving a
great impression of slender height from a distance. The house,
now abandoned and shut up, approximates to a modification of
the L-plan, with main block lying roughly east and west, the wing
projecting southwards at the east end, and a slender stair-tower
rising to a gabled roof midway along the north front. There are
five storeys beneath the steeply-pitched roof. The gables of the
main house and stair-tower are crowstepped, those of the wing
are not. The walling is harled, and the ground floor windows
are small and few. On my visit it was impossible to obtain access
to the interior, but it seemed probable that the basement was
vaulted. If there are shot-holes or other features they are covered
by the harling. It is a pity that this fine house should be thus
deserted and not in good condition; but history might possibly
repeat itself, for we read in a gazetteer of 1844, that Freswick is
'an ancient mansion, not inhabited for many years and now almost
in a ruinous state'. Obviously it has been restored and occupied
since then, whatever its state today.

This has long been a lairdship of the great Caithness clan of
Sinclair, with the Castle of Mey, seat of the Sinclair chiefs, nearby.

But, for all that, the house seems to have been built by others, the family of Mowat. The Mowats were settled at Buchollie, near Turriff in Aberdeenshire, as early as the 13th century, and this seems to have been their main seat. But whether in the first instance they hailed from Caithness or Aberdeen is not clear, for they are said to have had a charter of Freswick from Robert the Bruce. At anyrate, we read of Patrick Mowat of Buchollie selling the barony of Freswick to another Mowat, Andrew, in 1549; and Roger Mowat of Drumbreck was laird of Freswick in 1635. They retained the barony until 1661, when it was sold to William Sinclair of Rattar. It may have been the new owner, or James Sinclair of Freswick who was laird in 1675, who built the extension to the house. There followed a long succession of Sinclair lairds, who in time came to own also the larger Dunbeath Castle further south.

## GIRNIGOE CASTLE

Dramatically and strongly situated on an almost detached rock promontory which juts into the Pentland Firth about three miles north of Wick, Girnigoe, with its twin castle of Sinclair strangely sharing its rock with it, is a much-photographed and well-known landmark. The two buildings are distinct, although so close, and it is the earlier, Girnigoe, which has survived much the better, Castle Sinclair being now little more than a single lofty fang of masonry.

Girnigoe, dating from the late 15th century, is unusual in a number of ways. Its plan, largely dictated by the site, is E-shaped, with the main block lying north and south and two wings projecting eastwards, that on the north side being much the larger and projecting further. A very narrow space is left between. These two wings have been extended, later, to use up the rest of the promontory eastwards, but of these buildings little remains. To the west was a fortified courtyard, for here was the only access, and it is in this courtyard area that, in 1606, Castle Sinclair was erected. This forecourt was protected by a gatehouse and drawbridge, a deep ditch cutting off the promontory's neck here. Between promontory and mainland, to the south, is a deep geo, or voe, which partly dries out at low water, and here is situated a small postern gate. For security reasons this opens on to a sunken trench between courtyard and keep, which trench makes an abrupt and alarming drop at its north end into the sea far below, to discourage any rushed attack.

The main block rises to five storeys, and with the south or stair-wing, probably formed the original L-shaped building, to which the larger north wing, a storey higher, was added. Owing to the uneven nature of the site, the main block basement is a storey lower than that of the wings, and contains a vaulted dungeon and well-chamber, Above were two more vaulted guard-rooms. The foot of the stair-wing contained the door and entry passage, protected by two splayed gunloops, and the basement of the north wing housed the vaulted kitchen, this having a private stairway in the thickness of the west wall to the Hall above. The great chimney-stack, for the kitchen flue, is a notable feature of the roofline, this east gable being nine feet thick. The Hall is a fine chamber, 30 by 19 feet, and occupies the first floor of the main block. It was provided with a large fireplace, and an unusual heraldically-decorated oriel window, facing west, with the arms of the earldom of Caithness. There has been a *bretache*, or external timber gallery for defence, projecting over the sea on the north walling, at this level, corbels for which remain. A similar provision on the south side, over the geo, is at a higher level. There was a private room off, in the north wing, with a trap door down through the kitchen vault, and a door in the east wall giving access to the parapet-walk of the curtain-walling which enclosed the site on this side. A private stair rose in the north-east angle.

In 1455 William Sinclair, 3rd Earl of Orkney, was compelled by James the Third to resign the earldom, which he had held of the King of Denmark, on it being ceded to Scotland as security for the unpaid dowry of the Danish Princess Margaret. He was created Earl of Caithness instead. His second son succeeded, and probably built Girnigoe; and thereafter the castle was in a constant stir, in the stormy history of that line. Perhaps most grim of events that took place here was the imprisonment in 1571 by George, 4th Earl, of his son and heir, John, Master of Caithness, whom he suspected of plotting against him. He was kept captive in the dungeons for seven long years, and eventually died mad, when fed on salt beef and denied water. The Earl was a supporter of Mary Queen of Scots, and chairman of the jury which acquitted Bothwell of Darnley's murder. He had several sons, the most celebrated of whom was George Sinclair of Mey, Chancellor of Caithness. Cromwell planted a garrison of 70 foot and 15 horse in Girnigoe. The castle was attacked in 1679 by Sinclair of Keiss, when in the possession of Campbell of Glenorchy, who had claimed the earldom by an extraordinary arrangement as principal creditor of the bankrupt 10th Earl. Keiss, who badly damaged the building, whereafter it was deserted, was the heir of line, and managed to get back the earldom, Campbell being created 1st Earl of Breadalbane.

## KEISS CASTLE

Perched dizzily on the very edge of a beetling cliff above the sea, like so many other Caithness castles, Keiss stands on a promontory of rock 8 miles north-east of Wick, with its modern successor inland close by. It is a tall and impressive but not very large fortalice of the late 16th century, now roofless, but comparatively entire to the wallhead save at the north-east corner, which has fallen away. The building conforms to the Z-plan, with a main block lying north and south and round towers rising at the north-west and south-east angles. That to the north-west is the stair-tower, and is corbelled out to the square at its top to form a watch-chamber. The south-west corner of the main block is crowned by a circular angle-turret, with shot-holes; and a small stair-turret rises above second-floor level on the north front, supported on chequered corbelling. The walls rise to four storeys and an attic and are not very thick, for the period, averaging only about 3 feet 3 inches. The windows are small, and one at second-floor level

[93]

facing south-west is enriched by carving on the sill. A heraldic panel bearing the Sinclair arms was removed from Keiss to Barrock House.

Internally the building is completely ruinous. The basement was vaulted and the main stairway was comparatively wide. The Hall was, as usual, on the first floor, with domestic accommodation above.

Keiss belonged to various branches of the great house of Sinclair at different times. Originally it seems to have been in the possession of the chiefs of the name. the Earls of Caithness, as it is mentioned as one of their residences in 1623. In 1638, Lord Berriedale, heir of Caithness, wrote from here to his son, the Master of Berriedale, remonstrating with him for his support of the National Covenant, the Master being one of the five commissioners entrusted by the nobility in favour of that measure with obtaining signatures throughout Scotland. The Master died of a fever, in Edinburgh, the following year. In 1681, George Sinclair of Keiss, a descendant of the 5th Earl of Caithness, by a second son, succeeded to the earldom. He died in 1698, and thereafter Keiss was acquired by the Sinclairs of Dunbeath, who also stemmed from the main Caithness line.

# CASTLE OF MEY (or BARROGILL)

In an exposed position and with but token shelter from its wind-blown trees—not a common sight in Caithness—the Castle of Mey stands some 15 miles east of Thurso, looking out over the Pentland Firth, unlike so many of the local castles, some way back from the sea. In recent years it has achieved a new fame as the Queen Mother's northern home; but it has a long and stirring history as a seat of the Sinclair Earls of Caithness, themselves the successors of the Earls of Orkney, 'the lordly line of high St. Clair'.

Although much altered and somewhat spoiled in aspect by the 19th-century 'anglicised' heightening and crenellating of the angle-turrets, the building is basically an authentic fortalice of the late 16th century, Z-planned, with the main block lying east and west, a square wing projecting at the south-west end and a smaller square stair-tower to the north-east, stair-turrets rising within the re-entrants above first-floor level. The main block contains three storeys and an attic, with the wings rising a storey higher. The angle-turrets, carried on chequered corbelling, are in some cases two-storeyed. An unusual feature is the extra-massive chimney-stack, almost as thick as a small tower, which rises at the east end of the main block, and containing double sets of flues. The walls are thick, and well provided with gunloops. Many of the windows have been enlarged. There was a courtyard, enclosed by curtain-walls, to the north.

The original entrance was in the northern re-entrant and opened on to the main stair-foot, and so to a vaulted passage which gives access to the three vaulted chambers of the main block basement. One of these was the wine-cellar, and that to the east the old kitchen, with a great fireplace 12 feet wide by 6 feet deep, providing an ingleneuk, and served by the aforementioned enormous chimney. Another vaulted chamber in the foot of the south-west tower admits to the foot of a secondary stair in the southern re-entrant. On the first floor, as usual, was the Hall, later the dining-room, a handsome apartment of 40 by 18 feet, with a private room off to the east, over the kitchen, and another in the south-west tower. There was ample sleeping accommodation higher.

In 1566 George Sinclair, 4th Earl of Caithness, acquired the barony of Mey from the Bishop of Caithness, and began building the castle the following year. He was Justiciar of Caithness and Sutherland, and chairman of the jury which acquitted Bothwell of the murder of Darnley. His grandson George, the 5th or

Wicked Earl, completed the building. *His* grandson, the 6th Earl, got into great financial difficulties, and his principal creditor, Sir John Campbell of Glenorchy, to whom he was said to have owed over a million merks, on the Earl's death in 1676, married the widowed Countess (herself a Campbell) and took over the estates, getting a grant of the earldom. This was disputed by George Sinclair of Keiss, however, second son of the 5th Earl, heir male, and after long contest and actual warfare, the King and Privy Council finding in Sinclair's favour, forced the Campbell to relinquish the earldom, creating him instead Earl of Breadalbane— the origin of that title. The Sinclairs regained Mey and continued to play a foremost part in the troubled history of Caithness. Here, in 1650, was long confined Macleod of Assynt, who betrayed the great Marquis of Montrose to his death, after Carbisdale.

The castle, for long called Barrogill, after a period of neglect, was bought by H.M. the Queen Mother some years ago, and restored.

# DUNBARTONSHIRE

## DARLEITH HOUSE

Set above a ravine in the pleasant Lennox foothill country between the Clyde estuary and Loch Lomond, about 3 miles north
of Cardross, Darleith is a large mansion now used for institutional
purposes but which incorporates an early fortalice of the 16th
and 17th centuries, As is to be expected, the ancient portions are
those in a defensive position flanking the steep drop, and appear
to have consisted of a modest oblong 16th-century block lying
east and west, to which a century later was added a parallel range
to the north, more than doubling the accommodation. In the 18th
and 20th centuries, large extensions were added to south and east.

Little of the original work now appears externally, and even
this has been much altered by the opening up of large oriel windows, and at roof level. The western gable is the only aspect of
the 16th-century work which has not been built against. It is a
three-storeyed structure which has formerly risen a storey higher
to contain a garret within the steep gabled roof. A circular angle-
turret is corbelled out at the north-west corner, and below is a
handsome heraldic panel bearing the arms of Yuille or Zuil, the
date 1678 and the motto GOD'S PROVIDENCE IS MY INHERITANCE.
A small buttress below is no doubt to provide strengthening on
the steeply-sloping site. The 17th-century extension abuts to the
north, at a lower level, and on its north gable is another and earlier
panel, inpaling the arms of Darleith and Crawford, flanked by the
initials I.D. and I.C. There are no other external features of interest.

Internally the house has been almost entirely altered to link up
with the later mansion. The basement of the original portion,
however, retains its vaulted ceiling, and thick walling is evident,
but external harling and internal plaster hide all details. In one of
the first-floor chambers of the 18th-century extension, over an
Adam-style mantelpiece, has been inserted a roughly-carved panel,

taken from above the old east entrance, which bears the initials I.Z. and A.F., for John Zuil and Anne Fisher, and the date 1676.

Darleith in the 16th and 17th centuries supported a family which took its name from the property, under the superiority of the Earls of Lennox; and in 1510 Earl Matthew is recorded as granting sasine to John Darleith of that Ilk. The superiority remained with the earldom however, for various charters under the Register of the Great Seal list Darleith amongst the possessions of Esmé Stewart D'Aubigny, James the Sixth's favourite, who was created 1st Duke of Lennox. In 1670, one of the many John Darleiths sold the property to John Zuil or Yuille, a lawyer from Inveraray, who made the second enlargement of the house. He was a stalwart Covenanter, suffering fines and two years imprisonment in Dumbarton Castle for refusing episcopacy. The Yuilles remained in possession until modern times.

The old roofless kirk of Darleith stands nearby.


## DUNGLASS CASTLE

This castle is more readily observed from shipboard on the Clyde than from land, for it is situated on a small promontory jutting into the estuary a little west of Bowling in Old Kilpatrick parish, now wholly enclosed and inaccessible within a large oil-storage

depot. The place is given prominence by the tall obelisk erected there to Henry Bell, originator of steam navigation.

The castle has been quite an extensive and important establishment with irregularly-shaped curtain walls, internal buildings, and flanking-towers, most of which are now ruinous fragments, crowning the low cliff-top. The building was much altered in 1735 when the Commissioners of Supply used it as a quarry for repairing the nearby quay. Certain features of the early castle remain, however, including a seaward entrance reached from a landing-stage in the estuary, above which are the corbels for supporting a protective hoarding or gatehouse. At the south-east angle of the enclosure is a small circular flanking-tower with conical slabbed roof, fitted up as a dovecote.

The buildings at the north-west corner are the most extensive. These apparently consist of a late 16th-century L-planned range, to which has been added considerable modern work, now in turn derelict. The 16th-century dwelling-house is two storeys and a garret in height, the walling harled, and with a two-storeyed circular angle-turret at the outer corner and a small rectangular tower to the west. The turret is carried on continuous chequered corbelling, on which is carved a rough representation of the Colquhoun arms with the initial c, and alongside a man's face—a highly unusual feature. The original main entrance to the castle, by an arched doorway in the north curtain-wall, flanked by narrow slits, still remains next to the L-shaped house. The interior of the building has been wholly altered to link up with more modern additions, and all is now in a neglected condition.

Dunglass was at one time the chief stronghold of the Clan

Colquhoun. From 1439 onwards it was the seat of Sir John Colquhoun, Lord High Chamberlain of the realm, and one of the
most distinguished men of his age. The north-west building
which remains intact was presumably erected by Sir Humphrey
Colquhoun 16th of Luss, who in 1592 was slain at Bannachra by
MacFarlanes and MacGregors as he went upstairs to bed, a
tampered-with servant carrying a light which intermittently
silhouetted the laird at the stairway's arrow-slit windows—
unneighbourly conduct but phenomenal shooting! The initials
v.c. said to appear above a doorway may refer to him.

## KILMAHEW CASTLE

Standing high amongst the foothills between Loch Lomond and
the Clyde estuary, about a mile north-east of Cardross and not far
from the house of Darleith, this is an ancient seat of a West Scotland branch of the Napier family, which held these lands from the
late 13th to the early 19th century. It is perched in a strong position above a steep ravine, and forms an oblong block, now ruinous
but surviving to the wallhead. The southern end has been much
altered and 'gothicised', but to the north and east it remains
authentic. It has been a tall keep of five storeys and a garret, probably dating from the 15th century, the walls crowned by the
usual parapet and walk, of which only the course of individual

corbels survives. Most of the windows, which have been small, have been built up, while more modern ones have been opened.

The entrance lies towards the north end of the west front, away from the ravine, and is surmounted by a wide lintel which formerly bore the inscription THE PEACE OF GOD BE HEREIN. This doorway is provided with deep protective bar-holes, and high above, at parapet-level, are the great corbels for a machicolated projection from which missiles could be hurled down upon unwelcome visitors.

Access is given to an unvaulted basement, with a great fireplace in the north gable. There is a well in the floor of the southern altered part of this ground floor, which was no doubt subdivided. The turnpike stair rose in the north-west angle, beside the door, but this has fallen in, and the upper floors are now inaccessible. The kitchen would be in the basement, with the large fireplace, the Hall on the first floor, and the sleeping accommodation above, in the usual arrangement.

The building is now, unfortunately, neglected and in a poor state.

## DALCROSS CASTLE

Once ruinous, this handsome restored 17th-century fortalice occupies a commanding position on the long ridge that lies between the valley of the River Nairn and the coastal plain, about seven miles north-east of Inverness, near Culloden Moor. Here it was, indeed, that the government troops were marshalled prior to that momentous battle. The castle was erected in 1620 by the 8th Lord Lovat, and conforms to a variation of the L-plan, whereby two wings join each other in such fashion as to form two re-entrant angles, for better defence of the walling. A square stair-tower projects in the re-entrant to the east, rising to a gabled watch-chamber provided with a circular angle-turret of ashlar. Three other gables are similarly enhanced, and crowstepped. A tall and massive chimney-stack rises in the centre of the east wall of the

northern wing. Many of the windows are provided with iron grilles, and the walls, which are of a warm red sandstone rubble, are pierced with many gunloops and shot-holes. The south wing rises to five storeys, an attic and a garret, while the north wing contains two storeys less. A lower extension was added to the north gable in the early 18th century, and still later stabling and offices attached to this. There is a well in the forecourt at the east side.

The entrance, from the courtyard, is in the foot of the square stair-tower, equipped with an iron yett and a draw-bar, and guarded by splayed gunloops. It is surmounted by heraldic panels showing the arms of Mackintosh and the date 1720—but this is an insertion. Nearby is a detached stone depicting the Fraser arms, the initials L.S.F. for Lord Simon Fraser, and the date 1620. The basement contains a range of small vaulted cellars, and a kitchen with a very large arched fireplace. An unusual feature is the vaulted passage which runs round the base of the turnpike stair. One of the vaults is the wine-cellar, with the usual private stair to the Hall above. This has a slight squared outer projection in the western re-entrant. The main stair is wide and rises on beyond the first floor. The Hall occupies the south wing and has windows on three sides, and the usual large fireplace. There is a small turnpike stair from it to the upper floor, for the laird's family. The apartment in the north wing, at this level, was apparently the laird's private room.

As has been stated, this was originally a Fraser house, but passed to the chief of Mackintosh at the turn of the 17th century. Another panel dated 1803 bears the initials L.M., for Lachlan Mackintosh, the 19th chief, who in fact lay in state here from 9th December 1703 to 18th January 1704, whereafter no fewer than 2,000 of his clansmen escorted his remains to their long-delayed interment in Petty kirkyard. In due course Dalcross was deserted and became a ruin; but it has been handsomely restored. The present owners descend from the Lairds of Mackintosh.

# DUNVEGAN CASTLE, SKYE

This, of course, is one of the best-known castles in Scotland, seat of the chiefs of Macleod, and situated on the sea-loch of the same name in the north-west of Skye, just north of the village. Unfortunately, despite its dramatic situation, seeming to grow out of a naked rock above the shore, and its undoubted authenticity, the drastic alteration and remodelling of its roof-line in the 19th century has so spoiled the appearance as to give the impression of a 'sham-Gothic' castle on the English model. Nevertheless one corner of the whole has been left practically untouched since the 17th century, that known as the Fairy Tower—as shown in sketch.

While the origins of the fortress, a Norse-Celtic dun, are lost in the mists of antiquity, the early castle as we know it consisted of the usual West Highland model of a high wall of enceinte irregularly crowning the summit of a rocky mound, with a square keep in the north-east angle, dating from the 14th or early 15th century. Much of this is still there under the alterations and embellishments, with the wing of the keep given a spurious over-high caphouse or flagpole-tower, and the whole dotted with small dummy turrets. There were additions in the 16th century, when the Fairy Tower was built to the south-east, with a lower building extending northwards towards the keep still later in the same century; and this was remodelled in 1686. In the 18th century the old keep was in a ruinous state and was replaced by extensions to the west of the Fairy Tower. Then in more modern times the sham baronial additions were made, and the late 16th-century lower work widened and heightened. Access was formerly from the Sea Gate in the perimeter wall, by a sloping passage 50 feet long and 5 to 7 feet wide; but this was later supplemented by a doorway at main first-floor level to the east, reached by a flight

[105]

of stairs from the ravine which protects the rock on that landward side. In turn, this was superseded by a stone bridge and modern 'castellated' porch.

The keep measures 48 by 35 feet with walls 9 feet thick, the rubble masonry being harled and yellow-washed. Its wing projects in unusual fashion centrally on the north-west front, not at an angle. The entrance from the courtyard was at first-floor level, with a machicolation above. The basement is vaulted, and the wing chamber was the pit or prison, reached from a hatch in its vaulting. An angled mural staircase rises to the north-west. The Hall on the first floor is now modernised as a drawing-room, and has a mural chamber off. There is another vaulted chamber in the wing at this level. Above has been modernised.

The 16th-century Fairy Tower rises four storeys to a crenellated parapet projected on chequered corbelling, which returns round only two sides, east and south, with a gabled attic storey above. The walk is drained by the usual cannon-like spouts. The windows where original, are small, and in the east gable near parapet level is one with a chute in its sill—an unusual provision. The tower has a vaulted basement, and Hall on first floor—for this was built to replace the keep's ruinous accommodation—with sleeping quarters above. A turnpike rises in the north-east angle. The lower range stretching north is interesting in having a late 17th-century balustrade above the 16th-century corbelling. It was of two storeys, with three apartments on each floor, the basement vaulted. The windows have been enlarged.

The history of Dunvegan and the Macleods would fill volumes. Leod, son of Olaf the Black, King of Man, acquired Dunvegan by marrying the Norse heiress, and their two sons founded the twin lines of the Siol Tormod, or Norman, and the Siol Torquil of Lewis. Ian, the 4th chief, in the 14th century, received the Fairy Flag, still preserved. William the 7th chief was killed at the famous Battle of Bloody Bay, during James the Fourth's campaigns to subdue the Lordship of the Isles; and his son, Alastair Crotach, or Crookback, entertained James the Fifth at a feast on top of one of Macleod's Tables, a mountain nearby, in 1536. He it was who built the Fairy Tower. Sir Rory Mor, 16th chief whose drinking-horn is so famous, was knighted by James the Sixth, and built the low extension. Ian Breac the 19th made the late 17th-century extensions, and in 1773 Norman, 22nd, entertained here Boswell and Johnson. Sir Reginald, 27th, was Under-Secretary for Scotland and Registrar-General, and his elder daughter, Dame Flora is 28th chief and famous the world over.

# ERCHLESS CASTLE

This handsome tower-house is remotely situated in Strathglass, amongst the skirts of the Highland hills, about ten miles west of Beauly, within its riverside estate. The present building is a tall, L-planned house of the late 16th and early 17th century, four storeys in height, with the stair-wing rising a storey higher, stair-turrets projecting in the re-entrant and north-west angle of the main block, and an angle-turret at the wallhead of the south-west corner. The gables are crowstepped, the roofs typically steep, and the harled and whitewashed walls pierced by gunloops and shot-holes. There is 19th-century work attached to the north, and a large modern oriel-style window has been built against the west gable.

The present entrance, in the south face of the stair-wing, is not original. Formerly, as was usual, it lay in the re-entrant angle, where it could be defended from shot-holes and by flanking fire from turrets. The basement is vaulted. The wide turnpike stair rises in the wing to first-floor level whereafter the ascent is continued by the turret stairs. The Hall is on the first floor, and there is ample domestic accommodation higher.

The lands of Erchless in early times belonged to a family known as de l'Aird, or del Ard. The heiress of this line in 1368 married

the son of Sir Robert de Chisholm, a Roxburgh laird who had been appointed Sheriff of Inverness, Justiciar of the North and Constable of the royal castle of Urquhart. Thus the Chisholms, a Lowland house, settled in the Highlands and in due course became a Highland clan, with their seat at Erchless. The present house was built between 1594 and 1623, when the chief was John Chisholm, Commissioner of the Peace for Inverness-shire. The castle, sited on an important cross-country route by Strathglass and Glen Affric to the west, was garrisoned by government troops during the first Jacobite Rising of 1689, when it was besieged by 500 of Dundee's Highlanders. By 1715 however, Roderick Chisholm was leading 200 of his clan to Sheriffmuir, in the cause of the Old Pretender. In 1745 the clan was still Jacobite and the chief's son and 30 of his men were killed at Culloden. The main line of the family ended in 1838, when the chiefship passed to descendants of the last laird's sister Mary, famous for her efforts to counter the evictions in Strathglass during the sad Clearances days. The Chisholms no longer own Erchless, but the old house is still occupied and well-cared for.

## KISIMUL CASTLE, BARRA

This well-known castle, one of the most romantic and indeed oldest in the land, rises on a tiny island in the sheltered inlet of Castle-bay, Isle of Barra, in the Outer Hebrides. It was for long centuries the seat of the warlike chiefs of MacNeil of Barra, and in 1937 the present 45th chief, Robert Lister MacNeil, an American citizen, bought back the property, estranged since 1838, and commenced the great work of restoration, now nearing completion.

There is considerable divergence of opinion as to the dating of this stronghold. MacNeil, himself an architect, who has access to clan information, dates the original curtain-walling as early as the 11th century, built on the site of a Celtic dun. This, he claims, was later heightened, and with the addition of chapel, watch-tower, keep and other lean-to buildings, was all completed by 1430. Other authorities however make it of considerably later date, despite the primitive appearance. The late Dr W. Mackay Mackenzie in his *Mediaeval Castle in Scotland*, declares that 'there is every reason to be confident that not one stone of it was laid upon another before 1427'.

Personally, I feel this to be a mistake. The original early castle, consisting of perimeter curtain-walling only, is entirely typical of the many West Highland castles of enceinte described in this volume, such as Dunstaffnage, Duart, Innischonnel, Skipness, Tioram, Mingarry, etc., all of which date from at least the 13th century. And as MacNeil points out, Castle Sween, over in Knapdale, also held by MacNeils, is accepted as having late 11th-century characteristics, and sometimes claimed as the oldest existing stone castle in Scotland; whereas there is evidence to show that Kisimul was in existence before Sween.

Be this as it may, Kisimul is a splendid example of a piratical Highland chief's stronghold. The first curtain-wall, irregularly shaped to fit the little island, was only 12 feet in height, but later much raised, with an entrance to the east. Within this enclosure would be rough and low timber and thatched dwellings. Then was built St. Cieran's Chapel, against the north-east wall, crude and small but in stone. The watch-tower, semi-circular on the internal side, was then added to the north, and still survives as the lesser tower of the castle; and the curtains were raised another 12 or 18 feet. A Great Hall was added to the west, some 45 by 20 feet, with central fireplace and thatched roof. Thereafter the Tanist's or heir's house was erected at the western corner of the enclosure, to be followed by the keep, or Great Tower, which then became the main feature. According to MacNeil, this was completed in 1120, although it looks later. It is square, five storeys high, with few and small windows, and has a 10-foot parapet, some of the crenellations of which are lintelled over like windows. The basement was a vaulted cellar, with trap-door to a storeroom

above. Higher was a sleeping-loft for the garrison. The chief's apartment was on the third floor, reached by an outside stair, which however required a removable timber platform for access to the door. From its entrance lobby a narrow stone stairway in the wall led down to the barrack-room, and from a window of the Hall another mural stair rose to the battlements. There are no turnpike stairs. The Gokman's House, for the keeper of the castle, and kitchen premises, were the last to be erected internally, though there was an external building, to house the crew of the chief's galley, erected outside the curtain-wall south of the keep, traces of which still remain.

Although the Clan MacNeil claim descent from Neil of the Nine Hostages, High King of Ireland in 397, the first of the race to settle in Scotland seems to have been Hugh Aonrachan, King of Aileach and Prince of Argyll. His son, 21st in descent, was called Neil of the Castle, who it is alleged started the building of Kisimul in 1030. Twenty succeeding chiefs added to or made famous this stronghold, in the following eight centuries, taking part first in the wars of the Lordship of the Isles and then in those of Scotland the nation, down to the hot-tempered General Roderick, 40th chief, who after campaigning in India, went bank-rupt when the kelp industry failed as a result of government policy, and was forced to sell Barra out of the clan. During that long period the castle was the scene of innumerable stirring events, being besieged several times during the clan wars, without ever falling. As late as 1675 a King's Messenger, with MacLeod escort, was driven from its walls when he came to serve a writ on MacNeil, the outraged clansmen pursuing and catching him thereafter, causing the Messenger to 'rend and ryve his writs'. The clan was out in the Jacobite Risings, and even in 1750 an agent reported to the exiled Prince Charles that MacNeil of Barra would bring 150 men to aid a new Rising in the North.

It is good to know that the castle is again the Hebridean home of the chief of MacNeil.


## MONIACK CASTLE

This is a most unusual house, probably of the early 17th century which has been very greatly altered at later periods, at the roof-line in especial. It is normal as to plan, an L-shaped building with a circular stair-tower in the re-entrant angle, this corbelled out to the square above second-floor level to form the usual watch-chamber. The tower however is much wider than usual, and its roof is not gabled but flat, and although the present parapet with crenellations is modern, it appears that the early finish must have been somewhat similar, although a little lower. There are two separate courses of continuous corbelling some distance below, and drainage-spouts for either a flat roof or a parapet-walk project at the level of the lower course. The renewed harling which covers the building hides any clues in the masonry as to previous features, gun-loops and shot-holes. The tower windows are uniformly small.

The main house provides its own architectural puzzles. The roof appears to have been lowered, and though on both wings it is now approximately the same level, the impression given is that the west wing is considerably older. It is of three storeys, with small windows, whereas that to the east contains only two storeys, and here the windows are large. Nevertheless the lower walls of this wing are very thick. Both wings have lost their gables and now have hipped roofs, which detracts from the house's appearance. The north front has been entirely altered, with a double bow-fronted facade.

The door is in the foot of the stair-tower, and above is an empty panel-space. Flanking it are two small windows barred by iron grilles, one in the tower and one in the west wing.

Internally the building is wholly adjusted to the later developments. There is no vaulting. The turnpike stair is wide and the newel notably thick.

Moniack Castle was, and still remains, a Fraser of Lovat house.

Archibald Fraser, son of the celebrated Simon, Lord Lovat, of the Forty-five, lived here. The earliest reference I have found to the barony of Moniack was 1576, when the laird was Thomas Fraser.

## MUCKERACH CASTLE

Overlooking the wide and fair strath of Spey from steep foothills a mile west of Dulnain Bridge, this is the moderately-sized former fortalice of the Grants of Rothiemurchus, now ruinous. It is a fairly typical late 16th-century tower-house on the L-plan, with a main block of three storeys and a garret lying east and west, and a circular stair-wing projecting northwards. This is corbelled out to the square above second-floor level, to form a gabled two-storeyed watch-chamber, served by a narrow stairway in a turret projecting in the re-entrant angle. This turret is somewhat unusual in being carried on a squinch, or supporting arch, instead of the normal continuous corbelling. A splayed gunloop is sited in an unusual position just above the squinch. The walls throughout are not very thick, and composed of very small flat rubble with dressed quoins. Most of the windows are very small, though those of the Hall are large. The west gable is badly riven; indeed the entire fabric is in bad condition, unfortunately. There has been an extensive courtyard, with subsidiary buildings to north and west, part of the curtain walling of which, and of a flanking tower, remains.

The doorway lies in the re-entrant angle and admits to the wide turnpike stairway. The stair has now fallen in. The basement is vaulted and lit by arrow-slit windows. There has been a large fireplace to the south, now much collapsed. The Hall, on the first floor, measured 21 by 19 feet, with windows on three sides and a garderobe in the angle with the stair-tower. The main stairway continued to second-floor level, which is rather unusual in a house of this type and size, with the turret-stair rising thereafter.

In 1583 John Grant of Freuchie (or Castle Grant, as it became) 14th Laird of Grant, granted to his second son, Patrick , charter of the lands of Over Finlarig or Muckerach. This Partick Grant married the Lady Margaret Stewart, daughter of the Earl of Atholl, and was knighted by James the Sixth, dying in 1626. He built the present castle by 1598. A lintel stone bearing that date, with the laird's arms and the motto IN GOD IS AL MY TRAIST, is said to have been carried off the few miles to Rothiemurchus when the Grants obtained that great property on the forfeiture of the Shaws thereof.

# CASTLE STEWART

This handsome early 17th-century mansion stands on no seemingly strong site, amongst the level lands near the Moray Firth shore some five miles north-east of Inverness, not far from the airport. The area, at the head of a shallow tidal bay, is marshy, however, and such could be as effective a defensive position as a cliff-top or promontory. The house, rebuilt by the Earl of Moray in 1625, is unusual in a number of features. It belongs to the E-plan, with a main block lying east and west, and square towers projecting southwards at each end, so placed as to form two re-entrant angles each, for better defence of the walls. These are lofty, the main block containing four storeys and the towers two more. The westerly tower has a flat platform roof, the parapet and crenellations of which are modern. The east tower ends in crowstepped gables and three conical-roofed angle-turrets grace its wallhead. The main north-east and north-west angles of the house are enhanced by most unusual two-storeyed corner-turrets of large size, corbelled out above second-floor level, to face outwards at an angle, these finishing in small gabled watch-chambers. In the northern re-entrants formed by the two square towers, are corbelled out above first-floor level tall, slender stair-turrets. The

western of these is now topped by an open-work crown of masonry, which is modern. The windows throughout are regularly spaced, of fair size and there is a great wealth of wide splayed gunloops and circular shot-holes.

The original entrance was in the foot of the west tower, in which rises the principal stair, squared and 6 feet wide. The door in the centre of the south front is of a later date. The basement contains a range of four vaulted chambers connected by a lateral passage, and another room in the foot of the east tower. The westernmost vault was the kitchen, with a great arched fireplace in the gable and an oven off it. Next to this was the laird's wine-cellar with the usual private stair to the Hall above. The straight stair at the east end of the basement passage is not original. The Hall occupied most of the first floor, a splendid apartment measuring 37 by 24 feet, with a private room off to the east, and a bedroom in the east tower. The second floor followed the same pattern, with a large withdrawing-room above the Hall, and here there are bedrooms in each tower, for the main stair rises in the west tower only to the first floor, above which the ascent is continued in the turret stairs in the northern re-entrants. There is another storey above this in the main block, and two more in the towers, with garrets, so that the house was exceedingly commodious. The large uppermost room has four corner chambers of two storeys, showing traces of old plaster cornices.

There appears to have been an earlier castle on the site, but the date 1625 appearing on dormer-windows represents the period of rebuilding by James Stewart, 3rd Earl of Moray. In his *Earldom of Sutherland*, Sir Robert Gordon refers to a dissention between Moray and the Clan Chattan, saying 'this year 1624 there got the clan to ane house which the Earl hath now of late built at Petty, called Castle Stuart, they drive away his servants from hence and do possess themselves of the Earl of Moray's handsome edifice'. The building is still the property of the Earl of Moray, in good order and occupied by a tenant who appreciates its quality.

## CASTLE TIORAM

Few examples so splendidly fulfil all the story-book ideals of a Highland chief's castle as does this, the former main seat of Clanranald, in Moidart. Set on a tidal island in the narrow mouth of Loch Moidart, about three miles north of Acharacle, amidst wooded hills and scattered islets, it crowns the summit of a rocky mound in spectacular fashion, dominating all. Like so many other West Highland castles, this belongs to two main periods, the early and typical 13th- and 14th-century wall-of-enceinte fortress, which consisted mainly of a lofty and blank-walled enclosure of irregular form, crenellated and seeming to rise out of the natural rock, with a keep and lesser lean-to buildings within, as at Mingarry, Kisimul, Duart and others; and 16th-century interior building, with a heightening and elaboration of the keep, the addition of open rounds and corbelling, and enlargement of windows. The irregular and uneven site dictates varying heights and faces in the five-sided curtain-walling, and means that the courtyard within is here on three different levels.

The entrance is in the north wall, with a machicolated projection above, for defence. The north-east portion of the walling is thinner, having been rebuilt. An outside stair against the wall to the north west, within the courtyard, leads up to the battlement walk, contrived by lessening the wall thickness. This is drained by gargoyle spouts. Subsidiary building has been added on three sides, to the south, with the keep rising high in the northwest angle. The basements are vaulted, at varying levels necessarily, but the upper floors are now inaccessible. The range to the south-east has contained the kitchen premises, with well and oven. The Hall was probably to the north of this, at the higher level.

Amy MacRuari, the wife of John, 7th Lord of the Isles, divorced in order that he might wed King Robert the Second's daughter

Margaret, came here with her dispossessed family; from her second son, Ranald, sprang the great Clanranald division of the house of MacDonald. The wronged lady built the keep and other work of the 14th century, within an existing rude 13th-century castle, and resided here. Thereafter Castle Tioram was the centre of continual turmoil, battle and feud, over the centuries, as was inevitable as the chief seat of that warlike branch clan. It did not escape involvement in more national upsets either. In 1554 the Regent, Mary of Guise, commanded Huntly and Argyll to assault it by sea and land, using artillery, and when the fabric was repaired in 1888, several cannon-balls were found lodged in the masonry, probably as a result of this action. No doubt it was after this battering that the 16th-century rebuilding took place. The chief then was John of Moidart, the first to be styled Captain of Clanranald. Again, a century later Cromwell's troops attacked and occupied the stronghold. During the Jacobite Rising of 1715, Castle Tioram was finally burned, but by its owner, the last Clanranald to reside here, to prevent it falling to the hands of the government troops. Today, although a roofless ruin, it is kept in good order and is a favourite objective of visitors.

# MORAY

## BISHOP'S HOUSE, ELGIN

This house might well be termed the small brother of the mighty Spynie Castle, in that it was the residence of the Bishops of Moray when they must remain closer to their Cathedral. But it was no mere town lodging, having all the features of a fortalice. Indeed, most of it was built about 1406 at the time when Bishop Innes was superintending the rebuilding of the said Cathedral, burned by the Wolf of Badenoch, and so much aware of the advantages of a fortified house.

The building has undergone many changes and vicissitudes. Originally it was a tall L-shaped house consisting of main block lying east and west, with stair-tower projecting to the north. Then, in the 16th century a northern wing was added, by Bishop Hepburn, to the stair-tower, and this, with the tall arched gateway piercing it, is the portion which survives, only the partial walling of the main block remaining, to the right. The masonry is good, the walls rising to three storeys, with the stair-tower a storey higher and ending in a gabled watch-chamber reached by a turret stair corbelled out in the re-entrant angle. The crowsteps of the gables are of the gablet type common in ecclesiastical buildings. The windows are small, and a very fine oriel, not now *in situ*, enhances the east front. There are a number of heraldic panels, some of notable quality, bearing the arms of Bishops Innes, Stewart and Hepburn, and of the Earl of Mar, son of the said Wolf of Badenoch. Here the Earl of Bothwell, Queen Mary's husband, was largely educated by his uncle, Bishop Hepburn.

The basement is vaulted. The main block contained the kitchen and two cellars. The wing is unusual in having, within the tall archway, a standing-place for horses, with storage cellar adjoining. The Hall, on the first floor, formerly had fresco paintings.

At the Reformation the house and adjoining lands were granted

to Alexander Seton—who had already received the lands of Pluscarden Priory as a 'god-bairn gift' from Mary Queen of Scots, at
the age of six. By 1581 he was called Commendator of Pluscarden;
in 1585 was an Extraordinary Lord of Session as Prior of Pluscarden, and three years later was Lord-Ordinary with the title of
Lord Urquhart. But this was only a beginning. In 1606 he was
Chancellor of Scotland and created Earl of Dunfermline. He was
a most notable man—not the least in that he managed, despite all
his other activities, to be contemporaneously Lord Provost of
both Edinburgh and Elgin. He was, of course, the builder of
many great houses, including much of Fyvie Castle and Pinkie
House.

This house was entire until the end of the 18th century, when
it was unroofed. In 1851 the Earl of Seafield started to pull it
down, but fortunately was prevented by protests, and the portions
now remaining saved. The building was gifted to Elgin, and later
restored largely through the efforts of Lachlan Mackintosh, the
Elgin antiquary.

## BLERVIE CASTLE

Set high on a bare and windy ridge less than three miles south-
east of Forres, the tall tower which is all that remains of the once
large Z-planned castle of Blervie is a conspicuous landmark. Indeed it is said that from its lofty parapets parts of seven counties

may be seen. It could be argued that, since this is only a portion
of a fortalice, it might be excluded from this volume; but because
it has obviously been a very important portion of the whole, because what remains is in itself so entire and in good order, and
because its extraordinary resemblance to nearby Burgie Castle is so
striking, inclusion of both seems well justified.

The remaining building is a five-storeyed tower, rising to a
parapet with open rounds and the usual drainage spouts, plus a
circular stair-turret finishing in a caphouse for the flat platform
roof. Only a fragment of the main block survives to the east, with
no hint of the former south-east tower—which clearly must have
been less important and massive, and may well have been circular.
The handsome Hall fireplace on the first floor survives against
the east wall of the square tower—although it was of course in
the main block—and is embellished with a lintel on which is a
weatherworn heraldic carving alleged to be dated 1398. This is
obviously a mistake for 1598, which date would suit the fabric.
The tower is well built of good coursed rubble. Indeed so strong
are the walls that when the main block and south tower were deliberately demolished for masonry to build the more modern
Blervie House, it is reported that many loads of wood and peats
were piled against them and set on fire in an effort to aid the process of destruction, but that the castle remained fireproof for
several hours. Vandalism is not confined to our generation. Presumably the north tower defied all such attempts and was left

intact. It is of excellent as well as massive workmanship. The walls are liberally provided with gunloops and shot-holes, six of the latter and one splayed loop defending the basement chamber alone.

The ground floor is vaulted, as is the first and top storey also—the last for the support of the flat platform roof.

Blervie, also at times called Blarie, Blarvie and Blairvie, was originally a royal property, originally it appears named Ulerin. It was held on behalf of the King, in the 12th century, by Alexander Comyn, Earl of Buchan. The present building however dates from no later than the 16th century, by which time the lands were in the possession of the powerful Moray family of Dunbar, descendants of the ancient line of the Cospatrick Earls of Dunbar, March and Moray. At the beginning of the 18th century the estate was purchased by one Alexander Macintosh, who sold it to William Duff of Dipple, 1st Earl of Fife, with whose descendants it remained.

The similarity of Blervie Castle's remains to those of Burgie two miles to the north-east, is remarkable, though the latter is very slightly larger and more ornate. Clearly the same hand had been at the building of both—and strangely, a very similar hand at the destruction!

## BURGIE CASTLE

About four miles east of Forres, the lofty tower of Burgie Castle rises, unlike nearby Blervie, from a small mound amongst what is now level woodland and probably once was marshy ground. Apart from this difference of setting, the two castles bear an uncanny resemblance, and now both consist only of what has been the northern tower of a large Z-plan building, with a tall stair-turret rising in the former re-entrant angle with the main block, which is now represented only by fragments of walling. Again however the Hall fireplace remains in the east wall of the tower at first floor level. At Burgie the carving on this now exposed fireplace lintel is still clear and distinct, not having been subject to the same weathering. It shows a heraldic composition bearing the arms of Dunbar with the initials A.D. K.R. and R.D., a defaced motto, and 1602 ZEIR.

The tower is six storeys high, with an ashlar parapet more intact than that of Blervie, with open rounds and spouts, the stair-turret rising higher to form a circular caphouse, access to the flat platform roof. The walls are supplied with numerous gunloops

and shot-holes, and iron grilles still bar many of the windows. An interesting feature are the many small hearts carved in many places on the stonework. A massive iron yett is still in position at the door leading into the vaulted basement.

Only a fragment of the main block walling remains, but enough to show that it was lower than the tower. The castle stands within a fine pleasance wall, with a well in what has been the courtyard to the south, and a lean-to roofed dovecote. The remainder of the building was demolished about 1800 for materials to build the present Burgie House nearby.

Burgie was church land held by the Abbey of Kinloss. At the typical and unsavoury manoeuvrings of the Reformation period, Master Alexander Dunbar, Dean of Moray, of the Mochrum branch of the family, himself an illegitimate son of the former Dean of Moray, managed to obtain the property. No doubt having married Katherine Reid, neice of the famous Robert Reid, Abbot of Kinloss and Bishop of Orkney facilitated the transfer. He presumably built the castle, He also acquired the larger estate of Grange, in Banffshire, from the same source, and his son Thomas Dunbar seems to have had two sons called Robert, one inheriting Grange and the other Burgie. Dunbar of Burgie defied Montrose in 1645, and the latter's royalist lieutenant, the Lord Lewis Gordon, in 1646. In 1650 he supplied victuals valued at £1030 to Charles Second's army, bankrupting himself in the process. In consequence he had to sell the property, transferring it to his kinsman Thomas Dunbar of Grange. His son however did not accept the validity of this proceeding, and seized Burgie Castle by force in 1668, threatening to burn it down rather than leave thereafter. The outcome of this family feud is not revealed.

## COXTON TOWER

Standing out as something of a landmark, on rising ground three miles east of Elgin, Coxton is a small but especially interesting fortalice, no longer inhabited but fortunately still in a fair state of preservation. Giving an appearance of greater antiquity than the accepted dating, it is a building of the first half of the 17th century, built with a notably keen eye to security—perhaps an apt enough commentary on the times.

The tower is square on plan, and the walls, up to five feet in thickness, rise four storeys to the eaves, all ceilings being vaulted, and the vaults set at right angles, one above another—a most unusual provision. The roof itself is of stone slabs, carried steeply on a pointed vault, so that the house is to all intents fireproof. Even the ashlar angle-turrets which grace the north-west and south-east corners are stone-roofed. There is an open bartizan corbelled out at the south-west angle, the north-eastern angle being left plain. The walls are roughcast, the gables crowstepped, the windows small, and there are numerous shot-holes. Iron yetts or grilles cover certain of the windows.

Although there is now a doorway into the basement vault, this will be a modern access. The original entrance is at first-floor level in the south front, formerly reached by a removable timber stair—although now there is a stone forestair. Above is a heraldic panel bearing the arms of Innes, the initials R.I. and A.I. and the date 1644. This gives access to the Hall, and to the stairway which rises in the north-east angle. A narrow straight stair led down to the basement cellar. Formerly the tower has had a courtyard to south and east.

Altogether, Coxton is exceptionally interesting, and of course very well known. Presumably there was an older building on the site, for in 1635 Innes of Leuchars and other members of the clan were ordered by the Privy Council to restore the property of 'umquhal Mr John Innes of Coxtoun' to his executors, also the 'charter-kists of Coxtoun and Balvenie as well as pay 1,000 merks for the wrong and insolence committed in the taking of the place of Coxtoun'. Innes of Leuchars was brother to Alexander, the

new laird of Coxton. There seems to have been other trouble in the family, for there was another brother, James, who against the advice of his father 'undeutifully coupled himselff in marriage with Mariory Innes, dochter to Alex. Innes of Cotts', an act which so offended his 'guidsir and faither that they mutually bound themselves to seclud the said James during all the dayes of the said Mariory's lyftyme and the airs quhatsumever gotten, or to be gotten betwix them for ever fra all benefit of inheritance ... be richt, tailzie, successors or ony other provision quhatsumever'. Not evidently a marriage of convenience.

Later, at the end of the century, Coxton was sold to the acquisitive William Duff of Dipple, father of the first Duff Earl of Fife.

## EASTER ELCHIES

Attractively situated on a high terrace above the Spey, on the north bank a mile west of Craigellachie, and in the vicinity of the modern distillery, this is a neglected and semi-ruinous small 17th-century laird's house which has been much altered and added to, being partly rebuilt in 1857. The plan approximates to the letter T, with a main block lying roughly east and west, and a square stair-wing projecting in the centre of the north front and rising a storey higher, to end in the usual watch-chamber. This is reached

by a turret stair corbelled out above first-floor level in the western re-entrant. The upper storey of this turret, which is of ashlar construction, has been renewed. Many of the windows have been either enlarged or closed up. The gables are crowstepped, the roofing steep, there is a good eaves-course, and the chimney-stacks have large copes. No doubt the original entrance was in the usual place in the re-entrant angle, below the turret, but this has been changed, and the doorway in the east face of the stair-wing is of later date. There is another doorway, below a central gablet, in the remodelled west front or rear of the house, with a panel dated 1700 and bearing weatherworn initials. There have been extensions to the main block both east and west, the former now being completely demolished, the latter roofless. The interior is boarded up and now inaccessible.

It is a great pity that this old house should be abandoned in such fashion when it could be made very attractive. It might have been expected that, restored, it could usefully serve the distillery management.

Easter Elchies was a Grant lairdship, like so many others in this neighbourhood. The first recorded of the family is Patrick, second son of Duncan, 15th Laird of Grant, of Castle Grant, a descendant of whom was another Patrick, Lord Elchies, the famous judge (1690-1754). In the Easter Elchies burial-aisle at the one-time Macallan churchyard, is a notable monument with elegant Corinthian columns, commemorating one of the lairds, John Grant of Elchies. In Latin, the inscription ends: '. . . and after he had, by constant practice of every kind of excellence, in sacred as well as secular affairs, acquired the distinctive mark of true nobility, being summoned by the Author of virtue, he departed this life 4th March 1715, in his 56th year, leaving this unique structure to be erected by his only son Patrick in token of due filial respect and just regret'. Renowned judge or not, surely self-satisfaction here reaches its apogee.

## WESTER ELCHIES

Only a couple of miles south-west of Easter Elchies, this companion house of the Grants is in an equally poor condition, though situated in an extensive estate. It is a larger house which is now derelict and part-ruinous, but has grown from the nucleus of an L-planned plain tower-house of probably the early 17th century, extended to form a Z-plan later in the same century, and much added to later with modern work. The old part of the house stands to the south of the whole. Its main block lies east and west, with a wing extending southwards at the west end. The additional wing, with its circular stair-tower on its east front, projects northwards, thus completing the Z. The original part is of three storeys, with the north-east wing rising a storey higher. The roof-level of the latter appears to have been somewhat altered and now oversails what was no doubt originally a conical roof to the stair-tower. The walls are roughcast, the gables crowstepped, there are copes on the chimney-stacks, and many of the windows have been enlarged. The east gable walling of the main block is extremely thick, and may represent an earlier incorporated fortalice, and a curious buttress-like excrescence projects at the south-east

corner. There is a shot-hole in the east wall of the original wing, in the re-entrant, now covered over by harling; there may well be others elsewhere. The ground floor of the older part is vaulted. The Hall has occupied the first floor of the main block, and there is ample domestic accommodation in the wings and higher. The interior is now in a very bad state. An old heraldic panel with the Grant arms has been built in above the arched entrance to the modern addition.

Wester Elchies in 1565 was included in the rental roll of the Bishopric of Moray, with the 'ferrie cobbill' on the Spey, etc., and was held by James Grant, a cadet of Grant of Grant, for an annual payment of £16 9s. Scots. By 1620 however it was in the actual ownership of Lachlan Grant, gained presumably at the dispersal of the Church lands at the Reformation. At the end of the 18th century it passed into the hands of another branch of this great family, Robert Grant being a scion of Ballindalloch nearby who had made a large fortune. He died here in 1803.

# CASTLE GRANT

Set high in the midst of a huge estate, in the attractive rolling woodlands of Strathspey about a mile north of Grantown, it is strange to find this great and important house, not only shut up but abandoned and in a state of dereliction. Even so it is impressive in its sheer size and height, though it can never have been a really attractive house in appearance. Empty and neglected, it conveys a strange impression.

The present vast E-shaped building has grown from an L-planned tower of the 15th and 16th centuries, which still forms the south wing. The remainder was added in 1750 and later, to north and east, five storeys high. Lower wings, now roofless, project still further eastwards at both ends, to enclose a paved courtyard, itself a storey above ground level. The original tower was tall and fairly typical, rising four storeys to a corbelled-out parapet, with machicolations. Formerly it is probable that there would be the usual single garret storey above, within the parapet-walk, but this has been heightened to form two-storeyed upper-works of the 16th century, presenting a somewhat unusual appearance. A stair-turret rises in the re-entrant angle, above first-floor level, projected on massive individual corbels, not on the normal continuous corbelling, and ending in a circular caphouse. The walls are harled and thick, and the windows of the old part com-

paratively small. The ground floor is vaulted, and a wide stair
rises in the wing to the first floor only, above which the ascent
is continued by the turret-stair. The Hall, on the first floor of
what was the main block, was enlarged by the Georgian additions
to form a great dining-room 50 feet by 30 feet.

The 18th-century additions need not concern us.

Castle Grant was long the headquarters of the great family of
that name—although it was not originally so called. Formerly its
name was Freuchie. The Grants were originally settled in Strather-
rick, in Inverness-shire, some say descended from Gregor Mor
of Clan Alpine in the 12th century. The first authentic ancestor
seems to have been Sir Lawrence Grant, Sheriff of Inverness in
1263. The family probably came to Strathspey on the collapse of
the Comyns, and the first of Freuchie was Sir Duncan Grant of
Inverallan, elder son of Ian Ruadh, or John Roy Grant, chief of
the clan and also Sheriff of Inverness in 1434. Thereafter Freuchie
became the chief stronghold of the Grants, whose representatives
seldom failed to take a major part in Scottish history. It was John,
5th of Freuchie, who on being offered the title of Lord Strathspey
by James the Sixth—who attended his wedding—asked 'Wha then
will be Laird o' Grant?' His grandson was in fact to be created
Earl of Strathspey by Charles the Second in 1663, but died before
the patent was signed. Thirty years later the next grandson,
Ludovick, 8th Laird, had his whole lands erected into the Regality
of Grant, and it was then that the old name was changed to Castle

Grant. It was Sir Ludovick (1743-73) who was the great builder, enlarging the castle to its present proportions, but not improving its looks in the process. He married the eldest daughter of the Ogilvie Earl of Findlater and Seafield, and in 1816 his grandson, Sir Lewis, succeeded as 5th Earl of Seafield, since when the lairds of Castle Grant have borne that title and used the name of Ogilvie-Grant. The present owner is the 13th Earl of Seafield, who lives at the Ogilvie seat of Cullen House.

## INNES HOUSE

At first glance, Innes House may seem as though it has strayed into this collection by mistake, so much more modern and palatial a mansion does it appear, and no fortified house. Yet to exclude it would be more of a mistake, for it quite definitely belongs to the period, the tradition, and the class of building here described. Much in advance of its time, and superficially ornate as it is, it nevertheless is basically similar to its contemporaries, being a 17th-century house in the old L-plan, tall, with steep roofs and dormer-windows, a square stair-tower rising in the re-entrant angle higher than the rest, to end in a flat platform roof which itself is reached by the usual turret-stair and caphouse. The walls are harled and adorned with stringcourses, and all the windows are enhanced with semi-circular or triangular pediments. This description could fit scores, almost hundreds, of other laird's houses of the period; it is only in the details and embellishments that Innes becomes unusual. Although not perhaps to be discerned at first sight, it has a great deal in common especially with Leslie Castle, in Aberdeenshire, which was built almost twenty years later—although Innes of course has no angle-turrets.

Internally the arrangements are more or less normal for the 17th century; hall and withdrawing-room on the first floor, private stair down to the laird's wine-cellar in the basement, and ample sleeping accommodation higher. Needless to say, a high standard of workmanship prevails.

Innes is particularly interesting, not only on account of its advanced architecture but because of the fact that the history of its construction has been preserved. The Laird of Innes kept the details of his correspondence and expenditure with the famous William Aitoun, 'Maister Maissoun at Heriott his work, for drawing the form of the House on paper, £26-13-4.' There is of course great similarity in style at Innes to the well-known George

Heriot's School at Edinburgh, the Renaissance pediments to the windows and other ornament being almost identical.

There have been some alterations and additions in later years, but not such as to materially change the aspect.

Volumes could be written about Innes and the exciting family whose seat this was, centre of a network of Innes properties and branches in the North-East. The line derived from one Berowald, probably a Fleming, to whom Malcolm the Fourth in 1160 granted the barony of Innes, being all the land, along the sea-coast between Lossie and Spey. Sir James, the 12th chief, entertained James the Third at Innes; William, the 15th, was a great Reformer; his son Alexander, 16th, was beheaded by the Regent Morton; the 17th chief resigned the chiefship to a kinsman, Alexander Innes of Crombie—which led to much trouble and a disastrous feud. This 18th laird was murdered by Innes of Innermarkie in 1580, in particularly barbarous circumstances. The 19th laird was put to the horn in 1624. Sir Robert, the 20th, was a prominent Covenanter, and created a baronet in 1625. Presumably he it was who built the present Innes House, which was erected between 1640 and 1653—for he welcomed King Charles the Second on his return to Scotland, at Garmouth, in 1650. His descendant the 6th baronet and 25th chief, succeded to the Dukedom of Roxburghe in 1805. He had sold Innes in 1767 to James Duff, 2nd Earl of Fife.

# SPYNIE CASTLE

Undoubtedly this is one of the finest 15th-century castles in the land, and while this is perhaps no testimonial to the piety of the great churchmen of the Middle Ages, it certainly is to their wealth, building ability and taste. For Spynie was the palace of the Bishops of Moray, and vividly it emphasises their power and state. The ruinous but still magnificent remains stand on rising ground at the south end of Spynie Loch, two miles north of the bishops' great Cathedral of Elgin.

The castle, which dates from various periods, has consisted of a great keep at the south-west corner of a large courtyard area, with square towers at each of the other corners, a handsome gate-house in the east front, and subsidiary buildings, including a chapel, erected within the high enclosing walls. Usually in such cases the original building was the keep, and the rest developing therefrom. Not so at Spynie. The castle was here before the great keep; indeed the gatehouse predates much of the other work and bears the arms of Bishop Innes, consecrated in 1406. We know that the keep was built by Bishop David Stewart (1461-75) who, having excommunicated the Earl of Huntly and other Gordons, was threatened by the Earl that he would come and pull him out of his pigeon-holes at Spynie; the prelate's answer was that he would build a house out of which Gordon and all his clan could not pull him—and this great tower was the result. Presumably the earlier work was less secure.

The keep, rising from a bold splayed plinth, is six storeys and 70 feet high to the parapet. The walls measure 62 by 44 feet and are over ten feet thick, save where they face into the courtyard. Unfortunately most of the parapet and above has gone, but there have been the usual open rounds at the angles, gables within the walk to north and south, and a caphouse above the stairhead in the north-east angle.

There was a curious arrangement of entrances at basement level, by one door from within the courtyard and another without. The latter would seem to be a source of weakness, but it gave access only to a narrow private stair in the walling which led to the Hall on the first floor. Presumably it could be easily defended—and provided a convenient private exit for the Bishop. The inner entrance led to the pit or prison, a large and most unpleasant circular vaulted chamber, some steps down, which shared the ground floor with the wine-cellar, and which boasted no window or other amenity save a narrow slantwise ventilation shaft. The

wine-cellar was reached by a private stair from the Hall above.

The principal entrance was elaborately secure, considering the postern door weakness. It was at first-floor level on the east or courtyard side, and was reached by a timber drawbridge from the top of the enclosing curtain-wall—an unusual precaution. To the north of it was the turnpike stair in the angle, and a guardroom in the thickness of the walling. The Hall itself was a fine apartment, 42 by 22 feet, with great fireplace and large windows with stone seats. An interesting feature was the series of five vaulted mural chambers, one above another, in the thickness of the west wall, each 6½ feet wide, and so just large enough for sleeping accommodation.

The individual corbels for the parapet are large, of three members. On the south front are three panels for coats-of-arms. The top one, to contain the royal arms, is empty—but the other two display the arms of Bishop David Stewart, the builder, and of the notorious Patrick Hepburn, the last pre-Reformation bishop, whose picturesque sins are well-known, and who was so hard to dislodge from his fortress. A further feature are the great ports for guns, which are almost too large to be described as gunloops.

Of the remainder of the castle less survives. The south-east tower appears to date from the same period as the keep, and though similar in style is less massive and a storey lower. Only one wall remains complete. Of the other two towers even less survives; presumably they were of earlier and less strong construction. The gatehouse in the east front, however, is fairly entire, and almost unique in Scotland in the fine quality of its design and workmanship. It was defended by a portcullis, and a small stair led up to the battlements above. In the curtain-walling of the south front remain the arched windows of the chapel. A spacious tennis-court lay parallel to this.

After the Reformation James the Sixth gave the lands to Alexander Lindsay, a son of the Earl of Crawford, in exchange for 10,000 gold crowns. He was created Lord Spynie, but James later prevailed on him to resign the property again so that it could be used by the Protestant bishops. During the subsequent religious troubles Spynie was frequently the scene of conflict, and General Munro besieged it and compelled Bishop Guthrie to surrender in 1640. The castle was held by Innes of Innes and Grant of Ballindalloch in the Covenanting interest. After the Restoration it again became the episcopal seat, the last resident bishop being Colin Falconer, who died there in 1686.

# NAIRNSHIRE

## BRODIE CASTLE

This highly interesting castle, which throughout its history has never been held in any other hands than those of Brodie of that Ilk, stands in level country in the Laigh of Moray about five miles west of Forres. It is a large, impressive and composite structure, extremely difficult to analyse architecturally with any degree of certainty. There is almost certainly a very ancient nucleus, for the Brodies have been settled on the site since the 12th century. Lord Lewis Gordon burnt the castle here in 1645, during the Montrose campaigns, and much rebuilding followed. The structure, as it now stands, seems to date in the main from the 16th and 17th centuries, with large 19th-century additions, although it is probable that the large central tower, seemingly oblong but actually L-shaped, may contain much work as early as the 15th century, as may a similar tower to the north-east, now almost incorporated in later building but probably once a flanking tower. Over all, the castle consists of the large tower, forming the south-west corner of the whole, with early extension to the east, and further developments to north and north-east.

The main tower rises four storeys to a parapet supported on elaborate decorative corbelling of late type, with a garret storey above, within the walk. Its northern wing however has been altered above first-floor level, probably in the 17th century, to its present plain gabled form. The parapet is drained by a great number of cannon-like spouts, and provided with an open round at the south-east angle, remaining square at the south-west, which is unusual. The basement, built on heavy boulder foundations, is lit only by narrow arrow-slit windows and provided with wide splayed gunloops in main block and wing. A fairly wide stair-turret is corbelled out above first-floor level in the south-eastern re-entrant angle with the gabled addition, culminating in a conical

roof which appears to have been heightened and renewed. The
eastern gabled addition, also probably of the 17th century, is one
storey lower, and like the altered north-western wing of the
tower, decorated with a stringcourse above first-floor level.

Internally, inevitably, there has also been much alteration. The
basement contains five vaulted chambers. The old kitchen, to the
north, has a great fireplace and bread oven in the north wall. The
Hall on the first floor of the old tower is also vaulted, and decorated with plasterwork, which however must date from after
1603 since it features the Tudor Rose amongst other symbols,
celebrating the Union of the Crowns. There is also Brodie and
Innes heraldry. The ceiling of the dining-room is likewise of
heavy Italianate plaster of the 17th century. Strangely enough,
the top floor of the smaller tower to the north-east is also vaulted,
to support a platform roof.

Brodie, as is perhaps to be expected, having been for so long
the home of a single family, is rich in portraits and other relics
of the past. The Brodies seem to have sprung from the ancient
Moraviensis line, and were first endowed with these lands by
Malcolm the Fourth in 1160. There was a Malcolm, Thane of
Brodie in the reign of Alexander the Third, and a Michael, Thane
of Brodie had a charter from Bruce in 1311. Alexander Brodie of
Brodie, the 9th laird, died in 1627 and left six sons, who acquired
considerable property in Moray. A grandson was Alexander, 11th,

the Diarist, who was renowned as a man of great piety, became Lord Brodie of Session, and was one of the commissioners sent to Charles the Second in exile at the Hague. His son James left only nine daughters, and was succeeded by a cousin, George, who however 'made siccar' by marrying the fifth of his predecessor's daughters. *His* second son was Lord Lyon King of Arms in 1727. Their successors have remained prominent in the life of the North-East down to the present day.

## CAWDOR CASTLE

This magnificent castle, one of the best-known in the land, is quite remarkably unspoiled, and probably gives a better impression of the contemporary appearance of a great fortified house than almost any other. It stands on an undulating site, in a large estate, about six miles south-west of Nairn. The selection of this site, near the joining of two burns, has a curious legend. Originally the Thane of Cawdor's castle was some distance nearer the sea, but for some reason a change of site became necessary. The Thane, according to the story, was uncertain where to build, but in a dream he was guided to load a donkey with certain gear, and follow where it led. It would bring him to an area with thorn trees. The donkey would stop under one, graze under a second, but lie down under a third. Round this he was to build the new Cawdor Castle. However pointless this legend may sound, the fact remains that in the vaulted basement of the castle today there stands the upright trunk of a hawthorn tree. It has long been dead, but is well-preserved. It grows out of the earthen floor and disappears into the masonry of the vaulted ceiling, which must have been built to take it.

To attempt any comprehensive description of this great house, in the space available, is impossible. Generalities and a few details must suffice. The building, now large and extensive, has grown round a tall and simple oblong tower, said to date from 1396, although its upperworks were added in 1454, when there was a special licence to fortify. It was surrounded by a deep dry ditch and reached by a drawbridge—both of which still apply. Later accommodation was erected on all sides, in the 16th and 17th centuries, so that the whole now comprises a vast oblong of mainly three-storeyed building, gabled and embellished with angle-turrets and corbelled-out chambers, well provided with shotholes, enclosing three inner courtyards, out of which the tall keep towers.

Across the drawbridge a massive iron yett under a belfry, admits to the outer court. The yett was brought from Lochindorb Castle, in upland Moray, which an early Lord of Cawdor was ordered to destroy. The keep is four storeys and a garret in height, with very thick walls and small windows—though even so these have been enlarged and regularised in the 17th century. A parapet rises flush with the walling, drained by the usual cannon-like spouts, and provided with machicolated projections for downward hurling of missiles. There are open rounds at the angles, but these have been raised and given conical roofs, in the 17th century, which imparts an unusual appearance to the skyline. The gabled garret storey rises within the walk. The entrance is now at basement level, from the northern courtyard, with a machicolation high above; but originally the main doorway was at first-floor level, reached by a removable timber stair, for greater security. Both the basement and the third floor are vaulted. A straight stair in the thickness of the north wall leads up to the Hall on the first floor—though this would formerly be a private stair *down* from Hall to basement cellar. The Hall has been provided with wall-chambers off, now used to connect with later work. A turnpike stair rises in the north-east angle to the upper floors. Curiously enough the old kitchen would appear to have been above the Hall, not below, judging by the sink and drain recently uncovered

[136]

there. The handsome third-floor pointed vault was no doubt constructed to carry a flat platform roof for the keep, but this has
been altered as described. The chamber is now a very fine room.

Elsewhere in the later wings there are a great many features of
interest, including an iron-yetted postern door to the moat, at the
north-east angle; and a squared angle-turret, or angle-chamber,
corbelled out at the north-west corner of the range, with shot-hole
—though this projection appears to be of earlier workmanship
than the 1660-70 period in which Sir Hugh Campbell of Cawdor
remodelled and enlarged these wings. There are some fine 17th-
century renaissance fireplaces, including an especially interesting
one depicting a fox smoking a pipe, a monkey blowing a horn,
a cat playing a fiddle and a mermaid strumming a harp. The date
1511—before the discovery of tobacco—which appears on this
work, is recut and commemorates the famous marriage of Muriel,
heiress of the 7th Thane of Cawdor, with Sir John Campbell,
third son of Argyll. Their initials appear in the old Hall.

The castle is splendidly maintained by the present Earl of
Cawdor, and is a treasure-house of portraits, furnishings and other
works of art. Of especial interest are the magnificent tapestries
which Lady Cawdor is herself, at enormous labour, cleaning and
restoring.

The 1st Thane of Cawdor was of the family of Hostiarius, or
royal Doorward, who assumed the name of Calder when granted
these lands by Alexander the Second in 1236—part of MacBeths
Nairn estates. These Thanes were constables of the royal domains,
and resided officially at the Castle of Nairn, this being their private
castle. The 3rd Thane was killed by Sir Alexander Rait, of nearby
Rait Castle. It was the 5th Thane who built the present keep, and
the licence for so doing, from James the Second, is still extant.
In Latin, it gives '. . . full and free faculty and special licence to
erect his castle of Cawdor and fortify it with walls, ditches, and
equip the summit of the same with turrets and means of defence,
with warlike provision and strengths etc.; with feus, rights, cus-
toms, privileges pertaining to a castle . . . according to the custom
of our realm. Provided however that the said castle be always
open and ready to us, our heirs and successors . . . and that we
have always free entry and exit without difficulty or obstacle. . . .'

The story of how Muriel, heiress of Cawdor, was kidnapped
from Lady Kilravock's (her grandmother) keeping, in 1499, by
Campbell of Inverliver, on the orders of Argyll, at the cost of all
six of Inverliver's sons, is too well known to repeat here. The
present Earl is descended from this much fought-over heiress.

# KILRAVOCK CASTLE

This impressive and composite castle of the Roses, dating from the 15th and the 17th centuries, stands amidst a large estate, on a rocky bank above the meadows of the River Nairn, about seven miles south-west of Nairn. The original fortalice, a simple, free-standing oblong tower, or keep, rises to the east of the present range of building, and dates from 1460, when Huchone de Ross, 7th Baron, was given royal licence 'to fund, big ande upmak a toure of fens with Barmekin ande bataling upon quhat place of strynth him best likis within the Barony of Kylrawok'.

This massive tower, of coursed rubble 7 feet thick, rises five storeys to a simple parapet on individual corbels, topped by a gabled garret storey. There are open rounds at the angles, save to the south-west, where rises the turnpike stair, surmounted at parapet level by a squared caphouse. The windows throughout are small. In the 17th century the castle was much enlarged. First, a square stair-wing, rising to a gabled roof, was built abutting the south-west corner. Then, to the west of this addition, the main southern 17th-century five storey-block was erected, with a steep gabled roof, a semi-circular stair-turret corbelled out above main first-floor level in the centre of the south front, and another stair

in a squared projection, hardly to be called a tower, rising at the extreme south-west angle. Later and lower work was added, in something of a clutter, to the south-east and north-west.

The original door to the keep was at the foot of the stair in the south-west angle, now enclosed by the square wing. It was defended by a wide splayed gunloop from its basement passage. There are other shot-holes elsewhere. The basement is vaulted and there are wall-chambers in the thickness of the masonry. There is a high window above the Hall fireplace, on the first floor. The basement of the south block is also vaulted and contains a range of three cellars, with a vaulted access passage to the north. As there was no similar corridor on the upper floors, and the rooms take up the full width of the house, the two projecting stair-turrets to the south are necessary for access.

There is some dispute as to the origins of this ancient family of Rose of Kilravock. One suggestion is that they are descended from the ancient Celtic Earls of Ross; another that they spring from the Norman de Roos family. Formerly they were designated 'of Geddes', which lies about five miles nearer Nairn. A Hugo de Roos, Dominus de Geddes, was witness for Sir John Bisset of Lovat, of the foundation charter of Beauly Priory in 1219. His son, another Hugh, married the heiress grand-daughter of the said Bisset, and so acquired the lands of Kilravock. They were erected into a barony for still another Hugh Rose in 1474, by James the Third. Hugh, 10th in succession, in 1545 purchased much land from the infamous Bishop Hepburn of Moray, who was busy anticipating the Reformation and lining his own pockets. This laird, in a submission between two quarrelling neighbours, signed himself as 'Hutcheon Rose of Kilravock, an honest man ill-guided between you baith'.

Mary Queen of Scots visited Kilravock in 1562, during her progress into the North to bring down the power of Gordon. Hugh, 16th laird, entertained Charles Edward here, two days before Culloden, and played a minuet for the Prince on his violin; and the Duke of Cumberland, who came the day after, remarked that he understood that the laird had been entertaining his cousin —but for once seems to have exacted no vengeance, perhaps because one of Rose's daughters was married to Duncan Forbes of Culloden. Robert Burns was here in 1787.

Happily, the Roses are still at Kilravock.

# ORKNEY

## EARL'S PALACE, KIRKWALL

This famous building, described by Scott in *The Pirate*, standing close to St. Magnus Cathedral in the Orkney capital, though long a roofless ruin, is complete to the wallhead and accepted as one of the finest examples of castellated Renaissance architecture in all Scotland. Like Scalloway Castle in Shetland, it was built by the notorious Patrick Stewart, Earl of Orkney, at the start of the 17th century, and displays the strong French influence which was bearing on Scotland at that period, brought in by Mary of Guise and her daughter Mary Queen of Scots, grandfather's wife and aunt respectively of the Earl, though on the other side of the blanket.

The building is large and E-shaped, the main block, lying north and south, being some 90 feet long by 30 wide, the south wing extending westwards for 45 feet and the shorter north wing for 26 feet, of a height of two storeys and an attic. The walls are of the typical Orkney narrow flagstone, with warmer freestone dressings. Circular angle-turrets grace the western angles of both wings, and a special feature is the series of projecting windows of the main block at first-floor level, three bays to the east and two fine oriels to the west, mullioned, semi-circular and polygonal, and all most handsome. The gables are crowstepped, the roofs have been steep, and there is much decorative stonework, heraldic panels, stringcourses and mouldings. Also many shot-holes, circular and quatrefoil. There has been a courtyard to the west.

The entrance is in the south wing, in the re-entrant angle, by a splendid doorway enriched by Doric columns and carved work, with a series of panels above, largely weatherworn but showing the royal arms at the top. The door admits to a vaulted vestibule, with a wide scale-and-platt stairway to the right, and a very long corridor to the left running along the west side of the main block and admitting to the range of four vaulted cellars, and to another

[141]

in the base of the far north wing. Five windows light this corridor on the west. The south wing, as well as the main staircase, houses a little dark vault beneath the stair, possibly a pit, and the vaulted kitchen at the west end, with a huge fireplace in the gable. There is a well at the southern corner of the long corridor, an unusual situation; and a servants' door projects nearby, down some steps to the south, another unusual refinement, with a service hatch opposite into the entrance vestibule.

The first floor, reached by the main stairway, contains in the main block the Great Hall, a magnificent apartment 55 by 20 feet, with an immense fireplace bearing the initials P.E.O., for Patrick, Earl of Orkney, in the west wall half-way up, and another, smaller, at the head of the room and behind where would stand the dais-table. The Hall is lit by two fine bay windows to the east and one oriel to the west. Beyond, to the north, is a withdrawing-room with bay and oriel windows and from it the first-floor north-wing room is reached, with access to tiny closets in the angle-turrets. A small vaulted chamber is contrived above the entrance vestibule, with garderobe and fireplace. Above the kitchen is a private room with a double aumbry, garderobe and fireplace. Small newel stairs in the two re-entrants give access to the upper floor, now ruinous, but which no doubt contained a range of bedrooms.

The Earl Patrick, whose splendid palace this was—though it originally bore the modest title of New-Wark of the Yards—sought more or less to convert his fief of Orkney and Shetland into an independent sovereignty, much against the will of the people—and of the Privy Council in Edinburgh, where he was in due course executed, his death being suitably delayed by the demand of the clerics that he might have time to learn the Lord's

Prayer! Nearby is another handsome building, of somewhat earlier date, known as the Bishop's Palace, but this is in too ruinous a state to warrant inclusion here.

## LANGSKAILL HOUSE

Situated on the west side of the small island of Gairsay, facing the Orkney mainland, this is an excellent example of the type of fortified house developed in the North Isles, where the tower-house, familiar elsewhere, is the mark of the incomer and aggressor from the south. It consists of low two-storeyed buildings on three sides enclosing a courtyard, the fourth or south side being barred by a screening wall, well supplied with gunloops. In this lies the arched gateway, surmounted by a heraldic panel in an enriched architrave. A parapet-walk topped this screen-wall, formerly reached from the wing to the east.

This wing, as well as being intact, is probably the oldest part of the house, incorporating an earlier building than the reconstructed mansion of 1676. Its roof has been lowered, and it probably contained three storeys instead of the present two, a long narrow building measuring 67 by 22 feet. A panel depicting the Lion Rampant graces the south gable, which has four windows, two of them enlarged. The doorway from the courtyard is in the centre of the west front, and has a moulded surround with, above, a lintel bearing the monogrammed initials W.C. and M.H. together with a weathered inscription. There were formerly two more external doorways flanking this—an unusual arrangement—but these have been reduced to windows. Over one is another indecipher-

able decorative panel. Each led into a large and unvaulted basement chamber, and these would be the Hall and kitchen of the establishment. The central door led to the former straight stair, now replaced, giving access to the upper rooms, altered by the lowering of the roof; but which an old inventory refers to as the blue and yellow rooms, a modern touch, and the 'schole' chamber and closet. There are two good moulded fireplaces here, one with a Latin-inscribed lintel and the other with carvings of a hunting scene, and the initials w.c. and m.h.

The west wing is now very ruinous and the gables have disappeared; but here also is an indecipherable panel, to the south, and a skewput bears the initials m.h. and the date 1676. There are now no buildings to the north.

Langskaill in its present form was erected by Sir William Craigie of Gairsay, who sprang from the Lothian family of Craig of Craigiehall. The m.h. initials refer to his wife, Margaret Honeyman. He died in 1712. Whether all the initials refer to this pair, however, is not certain, for there is a memorial in St. Magnus Cathedral, Kirkwall, dated 1620, showing the arms of Craigie of Gairsay impaling Halcro, and the initials of another William Craigie and his wife, Margaret Halcro. An earlier building was constructed either by the Muirheads or the Bannatynes, who succeeded the Rendalls as lairds of Gairsay.

Not to be confused with Langskaill is the House of Skaill, in Sandwick parish, which is also a late 17th-century house enclosing earlier work, and with a somewhat similar aspect though without defensive features. There were a number of other Orkney houses built on this plan of a three-sided enclosure with screen-entrance-wall, such as Sandside, Howan, Carrick etc., now either fallen to ruin or without features surviving.

## NOLTLAND CASTLE

Towards the north of Westray, near that island's only good harbour, rises this interesting and handsome castle of the late 16th century, added to later, and now ruinous but preserved. The original fortalice was a Z-shaped structure of four storeys and an attic, the main block lying east and west with square towers projecting to the north-east and south-west, the walls reaching 7 feet in thickness. The northern tower and the nearby section of the main block still rise to their full height, though roofless; but the rest has suffered the loss of the upper storeys— if indeed they

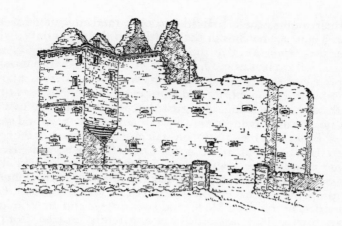

were ever built, for the castle was never completed. The upper
storeys of the north tower are projected on corbelling diagonally
across to the main block, in the north-west re-entrant, in a highly
unusual fashion, to provide space for a turret stair above main
first-floor level. The tower and this part of the main block are
finished off with a projecting parapet and open rounds. The
windows are small and the profusion of gunloops is notable. The
gables of the tower and main block show that the roofs have run
independently, at right angles. The first extension, of the 17th
century, was to the south, across a courtyard, and comprised a
lower L-shaped block, with corbelling for a circular angle-turret
at its south-west corner. Still later 18th-century work extended to
east and west of this.

An arched gateway to the east admitted to the courtyard. The
moulded door to the castle itself lay in the re-entrant angle of the
south-west tower, flanked by shot-holes and surmounted by an
empty panel-space on a stringcourse. The door opened on to a
vestibule and the main stair-foot, with a small porter's chamber
contrived beneath the turn of the stair. The central newel of the
very wide turnpike is most notable for its thickness and being itself
pierced by a wide gunloop. A vaulted passage leads diagonally off
to the right, giving access to the kitchen which occupies the west
end of the main block and which has a huge arched fireplace in
the west gable, with oven to right. There were formerly two other
cellars in the main block and another in the foot of the north
tower, with that next to the kitchen the wine-cellar, having a
private stair to the Hall above. These ground-floor chambers had
formerly timber ceilings to form an entresol floor at the springing

of their vaults, these half-floor rooms reached from the main stair. There are hatches in the vaulting to the Hall above, which gives the impression that the entresol was an afterthought.

The Hall is a handsome apartment 42 by 23 feet, with a moulded fireplace and stone seats in one of its windows. There is a pantry recess, with two aumbries and a gunloop, in the thickness of the north-west angle beside the great kitchen flue. To the east is a private or withdrawing-room, with stone window-seats and garde-robes. From here rises the turret stair aforementioned, in the angle. There is a bedroom in the north tower. The main stair rises no higher than this level, and its extra wide newel ends in an elaborate carved capital. A secondary narrow turnpike starts alongside, but probably was never completed. Above was a bedroom floor, and attics, in the main block, and two storeys and an attic in the north tower. This last attic was apparently entered from the parapet-walk.

Noltland appears to have been built by Sir Gilbert Balfour, brother-in-law of Adam, Bishop of Orkney, at the period of the Reformation when the Church lands were being distributed. In 1573 there is a Privy Council mention of the fortalice of Westray belonging to Gilbert Balfour. The castle was besieged and taken by Earl Patrick Stewart in 1592, for which he was punished. It gave refuge to the last surviving officers of the great Montrose's army, the following century. In the early 18th century it passed to the Denniston family.

# ROSS

## BALLONE CASTLE

Set in a strong cliff-edge position on the coast of the long, low, hammer-headed peninsula which projects between the Cromarty and Dornoch Firths, about ten miles east of Tain and one from Portmahomack, Ballone is a handsome example of a commodious Z-planned castle of the late 16th century, with a number of refinements and unusual features. It is now, unfortunately, in a very bad condition, the more sad in that it has been a very fine place indeed, particularly well built, with considerable ashlar, dressed stone finishings, fluted and carved window-surrounds and many gunloops and shot-holes. The main block lies north and south, rising to three storeys and a garret, with a circular tower projecting to the north-west and a square stair-tower to the south-east. Two slender stair-turrets rise in the south-facing re-entrant angles, though these are now much shattered. Corner turrets grace the other angles, and these are interesting, being of good ashlar work, notably well supplied with shot-holes which slant downwards for better shooting, and having stone roofs which are so built that they do not rise higher than the eaves course of the main roofing —an unusual provision. They are corbelled out on elaborate individual corbels, not the usual continuous variety. There has been a courtyard, with subsidiary outbuildings including a bakehouse and other domestic offices, to the north.

The original arched doorway lies in the foot of the south-east stair-tower, with a weatherworn panel above, in the re-entrant angle. There is a squint nearby in the stairway, to observe the approach, and another at the other side, from the main block wall. The principal staircase is a wide turnpike and rises only to the first floor, above which the turret stairs continue the ascent. Sharing the floor of this square tower with the stairway is a guardroom with a small vaulted prison off. The main block basement

is vaulted and divided into three chambers, the largest, to the south, being the kitchen, formerly with a great arched fireplace in the gable, which has fallen in leaving a yawning gap. The kitchen is also provided with an interesting pair of 'plumbing' arrangements—a water inlet and duct, with external basin, and nearby but lower, an outlet duct with internal basin. These are in the west wall, near the back door—which would of course have opened into the courtyard—and have been indicated in the sketch. The central ground-floor apartment was the wine-cellar, with the usual private straight stair in the thickness of the west wall, leading to the Hall above, permitting private access by the laird to his wine. The small chamber in the foot of the north-west tower is square, despite the circular exterior, and is not vaulted. The Hall, on the first floor, measures 30 by 19 feet, and has a private room off in the circular tower. The northernmost turret-stair opened from this room and evidently provided private access for the laird's family to the sleeping accommodation higher.

Ballone is said to have been built by the Earls of Ross. Since this earldom, which merged with the Lordship of the Isles, was forfeited and vested in the Crown in 1476, it seems unlikely that any of the present building was actually erected by any of the line. It may well have been built by a collateral branch of the Rosses, however, the main stem of which was settled at Balnagown not far away. Later it was occupied by the Mackenzie Earls of Cromarty.

# BALNAGOWN CASTLE

This ancient seat of the Ross family stands within its large estate about half a mile north-west of Kildary Station, in a formerly strong position on the edge of ground that drops to north and east. Although there is much old work included in the great pile of building, with parts said to date back as far as the 15th century, it is very difficult to delineate, so altered and added to has been the structure. Most of the building dates from the late 18th and early 19th centuries, but the majority even of this rises from ancient vaulting. However, a certain aspect of the early house is to be distinguished on the west front.

This is a tall gabled block of four storeys and a garret, with two slender towers at the north-west and south-west angles. The former of these is certainly of late construction; the latter may be also, beneath the heavy plastering—as may be the angle-turret to the south-east. The crenellations crowning the wallhead are also modern, but the bulk of this wing is ancient. The walls, rising from massive boulders as a foundation, are very thick, and the basement is vaulted. The windows have been enlarged and the unsightly arcading of the ground floor detracts from the aspect. There are now no shot-holes visible on the outside, owing to the plastering, but in the wall of the dining-room is said to be a recess, pierced by a shot-hole, on the sides of which recess drawings of

[149]

warlike figures in 15th-century garb are reputed to be seen. Unfortunately the author did not manage to view these. In another room a fireplace is said to have an elaborately carved lintel, dated 1680, with inscriptions and mottoes. Built externally into the south gable of the west wing, at basement level, is a monogrammed stone dated 1672. When visited, the great house was not being occupied, which seemingly has been its fate in other periods of its later history. There is in existence an old picture, showing the building as an L-shaped structure with a stair-turret in the re-entrant angle.

That history has been an exciting one, for after the death of the last Earl of Ross, the chiefship of that great clan fell to the Lairds of Balnagown, who were seldom uninvolved in the troubled history of Scotland. The 8th laird, Alexander, made a particular impact. Fearless and unscrupulous, his career of destruction, pillage and intimidation kept the countryside in terror. Continual complaints came to the Privy Council, and they were forced to act when they discovered that important tenants in the North could by no means pay their due taxes because they were so 'herreit and wrakkit' by Balnagown. This was in 1569. The Commendator of the Abbey of Fearn complained that he could not get *his* tenants' rents because of the laird's 'barbarous cruelties, injuries and intollerable oppressions and bludesched'—the said tenants taking their rents to Ross instead of Fearn. Alexander, summoned before the Council, failed to appear and was declared rebel. Captured, he was confined in Tantallon Castle. He died in 1592, but his son George, though well educated at St. Andrews, was little improvement. That same year, he with his brothers and sixty accomplices, took captive John Ross, of Edinburgh with violence and detained him against his will in Balnagown Castle. He was also accused of the slaughter of certain subjects, and with aiding the fugitive Earl of Bothwell, and was thereupon also declared rebel. His sister, Katherine, wife of Robert Munro of Foulis, maintained the family reputation by witchcraft and poison but though certain of her accomplices were 'brint for saim', the lady arranged a packed jury which acquitted her.


## CADBOLL CASTLE

Situated within the modern farm-steading overlooking the Moray Firth 10 miles south-east of Tain, the fortalice of Cadboll poses a number of problems. Ruinous enough to make inclusion in this volume questionable, it has unique features which make it especially interesting. It is a strongly built L-shaped structure with main block lying north and south, the wing extending to the east and a circular tower projecting at the north-west angle. Part of the wing has now disappeared, but the main block and tower remain to the wall-head. There has been a squared projection within the re-entrant angle facing south-east, in which, at first-floor level, was the doorway, but this is now ruinous. A roofless angle-turret crowns the south-east corner of the main block. The masonry is good coursed rubble. There are a number of circular shot-holes, and a splayed gunloop protects the doorway in the re-entrant. The original windows are tiny, most of those at first-floor level being merely cruciform slits for defensive purposes. The topmost window in the circular tower has a fluted moulding. The door in the foot of this tower is modern.

Especially interesting at Cadboll is the fact that there appear to be no windows or apertures for the ground-floor accommodation. Unfortunately, when visited, there was no access thereto either, for a great strawstack piled against the north side of the castle hid all features, and there seemed to be no access elsewhere to the basement, from within or without. Presumably it contained a range of vaulted cellars, unlit—something most unusual. The first floor is equally out of the ordinary. It is reached by the afore-mentioned door in the re-entrant by a stone forestair, formerly no doubt of timber and removable. There is a slot for a draw-bar, and an empty panel-space above. On this floor are three vaulted chambers in the main block, two lit only by the slit windows—again a highly unusual arrangement. The northernmost apartment's vault lies at right angles to the others, and it has rather larger windows. None of these chambers contains a fireplace. Altogether this first floor has the aspect of a typical vaulted basement. Unfortunately it was impossible to gain access to the upper storey.

The impression given by this high range of vaults and slit windows is of an early-type castle which has been added to and altered in the late 16th or early 17th century, when the angle-turret and entrance front have been built; possibly the wing also. A much closer inspection than the author found possible would be required to establish Cadboll's architectural history. It would look as though an early castelled structure had been destroyed, and a late 16th or early 17th century laird's house erected on the foundations.

A good L-shaped three-storeyed house of the late 17th or early 18th century adjoins to the east.

[151]

Early references to Cadboll, or Catboll as it was formerly spelt, link the lands with the nearby Abbey of Fearn. In fact one division of the lands was called Catboll-Abbot. In 1592 we read of William Sinclair, son and heir of George Sinclair of Mey, in Caithness, as being in possession. And in 1610, in the Register of the Great Seal, King James the Sixth confirms a charter of David, Bishop of Ross to William Sinclair, as above. Another division of Cadboll came to a family named Denoon, descended from a Campbell who took that name on having to flee from Dunoon in Cowal for some misdeed. One of this line became Abbot of Fearn, and his nephew got a grant of lands in 1534, his descendants retaining possession until the early 18th century.

## CASTLE CRAIG

One might well wonder—in viewing this remotely-set, eagle's-nest of a stronghold, so difficult of access part-way down a cliff-side, on the south shore of the Cromarty Firth twelve miles north-east of Muir of Ord and ten miles across the spine of the Black Isle peninsula from the cathedral-town of Fortrose—what caused the Bishops of Ross to choose this as an episcopal residence. We must come to our own conclusions about that, but Castle Craig was indeed an embattled bishop's palace. Since it dates from the 16th and 17th centuries, of course, it represents reaction to a very unsettled period in Church history, and the Bishops may well have looked on it as a citadel against the tide of Reformation rather than as a convenient house.

The remains today are ruinous and partial, but they indicate what is left of a large courtyard-type castle, with curtain-walling and round flanking-towers. Not much of these remain, but most of the central keep still stands, although its western portion has collapsed. It has been a tall, 50-foot high, oblong tower of four main storeys and a garret within the parapet-walk, but it is interesting to note that this parapet, projected on an elaborate cable-moulding and dog-tooth corbelling, with open rounds at the ends, crowns only the east wall-head. Possibly there was a similar provision to the west, now fallen away, but the lateral sides of the tower have obviously never had parapets. The small crenellation-like apertures under the eaves possibly represent something like a covered-in defensive gallery at this level. The walls are of redstone coursed rubble, and fairly well supplied with gunloops and shot-holes. Curiously there are no windows in the west front.

There are two doorways, one in the south, or landward front at ground level, and one to the north, opening from the courtyard, both guarded by gunloops. All the main floors were vaulted, which is unusual. The stair rose in the south-west angle. The basement has had a large fireplace with a great flue in the east wall and a water-basin and duct to the north, indicating that this was the kitchen. The Hall would be on the first floor and sleeping accommodation higher, as always. Small vaulted chambers have been

contrived on each floor, in the thickness of the east walling beside the kitchen flue. The upper floors unfortunately are now inaccessible.

Although Castle Craig was the residence of the bishops it is said to have been first erected by the Urquharts, Barons of Cromarty. The Bishops of Ross took a major part in Scots history, far outwith the bounds of their diocese, and episcopacy retained a tenacious hold on the area, with the bishops still in power there until 1638. Their final exodus was hardly up to standard, however. We read, in Spalding, that in March of that year schoolboys rushed into the cathedral as the service was starting, and taking all the prayerbooks, removed and burned them. The Bishop was much upset. 'He wes not longsum but schort at sermon, and thairefter haistellie gois to horss and spak with the Bishop of Moray, syne with the Marques of Huntlie and privateiy disgyssit he rode south to the King . . . ane very bussie man . . . and dost for feir of his lyf not returne to Scotland agane.'


## EILEAN DONAN CASTLE

This, perhaps the most photographed castle in all Scotland, occupies a tiny island at Dornie, in the mouth of Loch Duich, where that loch and Loch Long meet the wider Loch Alsh, opposite Skye, a position of great strength both tactical and strategic. It was long the chief stronghold of the Mackenzies of Kintail, chiefs of the name, and latterly in the keeping of MacRae constables.

The building as it now stands is very largely a reconstruction, for it was long an ivy-clad ruin. But fortunately there was sufficient left, especially of the keep with its 10-foot thick walls, to restore to something of its original appearance. The site was always recognised as important, and here was a Caledonian vitrified fort. In the 13th century the lands are alleged to have been given by Alexander the Third to Colin Fitzgerald, a son of the Irish Earl of Desmond, for his aid in defeating the invading King Hakon of Norway at the Battle of Largs. Some claim that it is from a descendant of this Irish lordling, named Kenneth, that the Clan Mackenzie takes its origin—though this is denied by many experts. Be that as it may, the original Eilean Donan Castle was a fairly typical 13th-century 'castle of enceinte' of the sort so common in the West Highlands, consisting of little more than a very high and strong crenellated wall of irregular outline, enclosing a courtyard in which lean-to buildings were erected. As again so

frequently happened, in the 14th or 15th century a rectangular keep was built at one corner, here the north-east angle, making use of part of the enceinte walling. This is the massive tower which, restored, now dominates the scene at Dornie, with fragments of the earlier enclosing walls incorporated in the secondary and more modern and lower building. There has been a flanking tower to the south-west, and an interesting water cistern enclosure connected to the courtyard by a sloping passage.

The keep rises three storeys to a gabled roof containing a garret, within a flush parapet. There is an open round at the north-west angle, a small gabled watch-chamber to the south-west, and conical-roofed caphouses on the east and west fronts giving access to the parapet walk; also a number of machicolated projections. But most of these features must be reconstructions, however authentic in style, since early drawings show little at parapet level surviving.

In 1331 Randolph, Earl of Moray, as an act of retribution and warning, decorated the curtain walls of Eilean Donan with the heads of fifty victims; and its continuing history was one of violence, inevitably, as significantly situated as it was and in the possession of so powerful and turbulent a clan. In 1504 Huntly took it, while quelling one of the many insurrections. In 1539 it was besieged by Donald Gorm of Lewis—but the siege was called off when Donald himself was killed by a lucky arrow fired from the castle. In 1719 it was the centre of the abortive Jacobite Rising, when the Spanish troops held it under William Mackenzie, Earl of Seaforth. After the Battle of Glensheil nearby, it was bombarded by three English men-of-war—which accounts for its drastic state of ruin prior to reconstruction by the late Colonel MacRae-Gilstrap this century. It is still the seat of the MacRaes, and now houses the Clan MacRae War Memorial.

## FAIRBURN TOWER

Standing high on a long ridge between the straths of Orrin and Conon about five miles north-west of Muir of Ord, this tall and impressive tower, although now ruinous, remains entire to the wallhead externally, and is an excellent example of the tower-house of the 16th and 17th centuries. It looks homogeneous, at first sight, but in fact dates from two periods, the tall stair-tower having been added in the early 17th century to the south-east of an existing and more massively built oblong keep. The walls of this latter, forming the main block of the present building, are of rough masonry, 5 feet 6 inches in thickness, rising four storeys and a garret to crowstepped gables. Two circular angle-turrets to north-east and south-west enhance these gables. The windows are comparatively small and there are a number of gunloops and shot-holes. There has been a courtyard to south and west.

The entrance is not in the re-entrant angle, as is usual, but in the south face of the stair-tower, the door being protected by two shot-holes in the west face of the tower, one being triangular, and by a gunloop with a wide squared and splayed aperture nearby in the south face of the keep. A large round shot-hole opens at first-floor level in the east gable. The stair in the additional 17th-century tower rose right to the top floor of the keep, and there ended in a small gabled watch-chamber with its own fireplace and chimney. The original keep stairway has been in the same south-east angle, the rounded recess for which is evident above first-floor level.

The early keep entrance was at the first floor, reached by a re-movable timber stair, and defended by a sliding bar, for which the socket remains. The Hall, on this first floor, had several wall chambers. A straight stair in the north-east angle led down to the vaulted basement chamber, to which there was no external door. Similarly-sized apartments, with garderobes, were provided on the upper floors. However rough the external masonry, which has been harled, the interior was well appointed, with arched window-recesses, moulded fireplaces and many aumbries.

[156]

Fairburn was a stronghold of a branch of the Mackenzies, so powerful in Ross. It featured in one of the 17th-century Brahan Seer's famous prophesies when, the building being used for the storage of hay, a cow managed to find its way in and up the long winding stair to the watch-chamber at the top. It was found impossible to bring it down again until it had calved—which event the Seer had foreseen as indicating the downfall of the Seaforth or Kintail family, chiefs of Mackenzie. A special train was run from Inverness with sightseers to view the event.

## KILCOY CASTLE

It will come as a surprise to many to learn that this fine example of an early 17th-century fortalice was formerly in a ruinous and roofless state. Restored, it stands, like Kinkell and Redcastle, at the neck of the Black Isle peninsula, on the southern slopes of the central ridge, about three miles east of Muir of Ord. It is built on the Z-plan, with a main block lying east and west and circular towers projecting to north-west and south-east, the latter being corbelled out to the square above second-floor level, to end in the usual gabled watch-chamber. Circular angle-turrets enhance the two opposite main block corners, and stair-turrets rise above first floor level in the two south-facing re-entrant angles.

The walls, of warm red rubble, rise to four main storeys, with the towers reaching a storey higher. The masonry is excellent, there are relieving arches over many of the windows, the walls are pierced with numerous gunloops and shot-holes, and there is considerable heraldic decoration. Particularly interesting features are the two very fine decorative dormer windows, one near the south-west turret on the main block and the other on the north-west tower; the manner in which the chimney-stack rising above this tower is curved to match; and the richly carved gargoyle rain-water spouts which project from the eaves of both towers, unusual where there is no parapet. The main roofs are slated, but those of the stair-turrets are stone-slabbed.

The original entrance was in the re-entrant with the south-east tower, protected by a gunloop, the present doorway being in the centre of the south front. Above are two empty panel spaces. The basement is vaulted and contains four cellars served by a vaulted passage along the south front. The easternmost chamber is the kitchen, which is provided with a stone filler basin for inward water supply, and sink and drain for disposal. There is also a service window, or hatch, to the passage. The central apartment is the wine-cellar, with the usual private stair to the Hall above. There is another cellar in the circular tower to the north-west, oddly shaped like all the rooms in this tower. The Hall on the first floor has a private room off to the west, and a small bedroom in the north-west tower, all provided with garderobes and aumbries. The lintel of the Hall fireplace is carved with three Mac-

[158]

kenzie shields, dated 1679, and decorated with mermaids playing harps, and with a carved greyhound at one end and a hare at the other. Above this level, served by the turret-stairs, is ample sleeping accommodation.

Kilcoy was acquired in 1618 by Alexander Mackenzie, fourth son of the 11th Baron of Kintail, chief of the clan, and the castle erected by him. His descendants in due course attained the dignity of a baronetcy, which however became extinct in 1883. Of this family came the distinguished General Mackenzie Fraser of Inverallochy, who was born at Kilcoy.

# KINKELL CASTLE

After being long in a bad state of repair, and deserted, this attractive modestly-sized fortalice of the late 16th century is now in process of restoration by its new and far-seeing owners. It stands in woodland, on rising ground at the base of the Black Isle peninsula about a mile south-east of Conon Bridge. It now has a rather unusual plan. Originally it has approximated to a variety of the Z-plan, with the main block lying east and west, a large circular stair-tower rising at the south-east angle, and a slender stair-turret corbelled out above first-floor level at the opposite north-west corner. The main block, however, has been extended at a later date, at the east end. The walls, harled, rise from a plinth or basement course, three storeys and a garret, to steep roof and crowstepped gables, the round tower rising a storey higher to contain the usual watch-chamber. There are a number of shot-holes and splayed gunloops, some uncovered during the present reconstruction.

The door is in the re-entrant, in the foot of the stair-tower, and is guarded by four gunloops. Above the lintel is an empty heraldic panel space. The basement contain two vaulted chambers in the original main block, reached from a vaulted passage at the south. The eastern apartment is the kitchen, with a large arched fireplace and a mural slop-drain. A small private stair ascends nearby to the Hall above. The ground floor apartment in the eastern extension is not vaulted. The turnpike stairway in the tower is wide. The Hall fireplace, on the first floor, is in the west gable, and has been decorated by a carved shield, now unfortunately defaced, and dated 1594. There is a garderobe in one corner here, and the windows have arched heads. The private turnpike in the turret rises in the north-west corner. The upper floor is supported

on good projecting corbels and has been divided into two apartments, there being two fireplaces, and two shot-holes side by side, presumably one for each room. There is now no garret storey, though once there would be; there has been some alteration of the roof level at an early period, and the stair-turret roof seems to have been heightened.

Kinkell was a property of the powerful family of Mackenzie of Gairloch which duly, in 1703, acquired the dignity of a baronetcy. In 1616 the Laird of Kinkell was before the Privy Council on a charge of rebellion, at the instance of Master Thomas Young. And at Kinkell in 1600 John Mackenzie of Gairloch, and his son, with Duncan Bain of Tulloch, subscribed an undertaking not to harm one Rory Mackenzie of Sligo. The building sank to the role of farmhouse before being abandoned. It is highly satisfactory that it has now been saved, and is in loving hands.

## CASTLE LEOD

This most handsome and commodious house, situated impressively on a green mound in its large and nobly-wooded estate, less than a mile north of Strathpeffer, is somewhat misleading in its looks, seeming at first glance to be both homogeneous and rather more ancient than it is. It was however built about 1600 by the famous Tutor of Kintail, Sir Roderick Mackenzie of Coigeach, on a modified form of the L-planned fortalice; but only shortly later, in 1616 if we are to go by dates appearing on the dormer windows, he filled in the re-entrant angle by building a large and high extension, to provide a wide squared staircase and additional bedroom accommodation. This portion, although apt to appear of the same period, is slightly higher, and is enhanced by conical-roofed angle-turrets and dormer windows, while the original L-shaped tower's wallhead was surmounted by a parapet and open rounds, projected on individual corbelling set chequer-wise. The sketch reveals something of this dual construction. The walls, seven to eight feet in thickness, with numerous recesses, rise from a substantial plinth or basement course, and are of an attractive warm red sandstone, good coursed rubble with dressed quoins. The entire building is well supplied with splayed gunloops and arrow-slit windows. Many of the larger windows retain their iron grilles.

The entrance is in the south-front, opening on to a terrace, in the filled-in portion of the L, the doorway being guarded by shot-holes and surmounted by a large and elaborately decorative panel with Mackenzie heraldic bearings. The basement contains the old kitchen in the wing, and vaulted cellars in the main block. On the first floor, the main block houses a fine Hall, 32 by 21 feet, with a large fireplace. A private room off, in the wing, is now the drawing-room. There is more ample bedroom accommodation than usual, on account of the addition.

The builder, the Tutor of Kintail, uncle and guardian of the young first Lord Mackenzie of Kintail, chief of the clan, was famous in Highland history and a remarkable man, achieving great things for himself, his clan, and the country generally. He married the heiress of Macleod of Coigeach, so gaining that property. His grandson was also an able man, Clerk Register of Scotland, and created Viscount Tarbat and Earl of Cromartie in 1703; and he consistently added to his estates until they included practically the whole of the former county of Cromarty. The 3rd Earl was forfeited for his share in the Rising of 1745, but the estates were eventually restored and a re-grant made of the earldom. Castle Leod is still the seat of his descendant, the present Earl of Cromartie.

## REDCASTLE

Redcastle, or Edradour as it was formerly called, is an unusual building in a number of respects, now unhappily fallen on evil days. It stands in a strong position on a slantwise and difficult site above a steep ravine, in a large estate on the north shore of the Beauly Firth, four miles east of Muir of Ord. The site has dictated a distinctly peculiar plan, so that the wall-faces to south and west are not at right angles. Included in the present building is the nucleus of the very old castle of Edradour, but this has been much added to and altered in the 16th and 17th centuries, and in modern times, making it almost impossible to give any clear overall description of the building in the space here available. The construction approximates to the L-plan, with extensions, plus a later tall, square stair-tower in the re-entrant angle. The oldest parts are the lower vaulted storeys to west and south, where the walling is exceedingly thick. Above these is mainly 16th-century work, the gables being surmounted by angle-turrets on fairly elaborate corbelling, circular at the south gable, squared at the north-west, and well supplied with shot-holes. To the north are 17th-century extensions, with a round and a square tower projecting, and on the gable here is a panel inscribed R.MK. and dated 1641. There is some picturesque buttressing nearby, required by the steeply sloping site. The east front has been considerably altered, and here lies the entrance.

The door is, and probably always has been, in the re-entrant, at the foot of the stair-tower. The Hall was centrally situated on the first floor, with a private room off to the east. Unfortunately internally all is now in a state of ruin and collapse, and sundry dormer pediments and other features lie around in the rubble and weeds.

This is one of those buildings where claims have been made that it is, or was, the oldest inhabited house in Scotland, based on Edradour's believed building in 1179 by David, brother of William the Lyon. Be this as it may, the castle was a notable stronghold for long. It belonged in 1230 to Sir John Bisset, of the family on whose foundations the Frasers rose to power in the North. The Douglases gained possession, and this was one of the properties that James the Gross, the 7th Earl, passed on to his illustrious son, the 8th Earl, who was stabbed to death by James the Second. His brother was created Earl of Ormond, which area included this Edradour. At the fall of the Douglases in 1455, nearly all this Black Isle area was annexed to the Crown. Mary Queen of Scots visited it in 1562 during her one excursion into the North. Just when its name was changed to Redcastle is not clear; its masonry is of the local red stone, but then so is that of its neighbouring castles. Like much else in this area, the property came into the possession of the Mackenzies in the 17th century, and the panel afore-mentioned indicates this. In modern times Redcastle passed to the Baillies of Dochfour. It is sad that it should have suffered such complete abandonment.

[163]

# LITTLE TARREL, or ROCKFIELD CASTLE

This small fortalice, now unfortunately in a bad state of repair, stands beside the modern farm-steading of Rockfield, in Tarbat parish, nine miles east of Tain, and approximately midway between Cadboll and Ballone Castles. It is an L-shaped structure, apparently of the early 17th century, although possibly containing older work, with typical steep roofing, crowstepped gables and substantial boulder foundations. The walling rises on a wide plinth to north and east, and has been harled, though this is flaking off. There are only two storeys beneath the eaves course, and a garret above, with no stair-tower or turret. The main block lies east and west, with the wing extending southwards at the east end. There are wide splayed gunloops in the west gable and the north front, and a circular shot-hole guards the arched doorway in the re-entrant angle. A modern forestair has been erected in the re-entrant, to a modern doorway at first-floor level, replacing the original internal turnpike, no doubt for access when the building was used as a farm-workers' tenement. It now stands derelict.

The basement has two vaulted chambers and a vaulted access passage, but the eastern portion of the main block has lost its vaulting and been much altered, probably when the turnpike stair was removed. The kitchen, in the south wing basement, has had a large arched fireplace, now blocked up, a stone water basin, and a large aumbry or wall-cupboard. The other vault to the west is only a cellar, lit by slits and the gunloop. The upper floor has suffered much alteration, save in the chamber over the kitchen, which retains two aumbries, a garderobe with its own small

[164]

window, now blocked, and a moulded stone fireplace. The only features of interest elsewhere are the position of the northern gun-loop, placed high, just under the eaves-course, giving the impression that the roof must have been lowered; and the sill of the first-floor window on the south of the main block, which has an inscription now weatherworn, lichen-covered and indecipherable.

The history of this little castle is difficult to trace, owing to confusion in the naming. It has been called Tarul and Tarradel, as well as Little Tarrel or Rockfield; moreover, there is a Meikle Tarrel nearby. To add to the confusion, there is another Tarradale in Ross, in Urray parish. In 1587, Tarradel in Ross is mentioned in the Register of the Great Seal, amongst other lands, in a charter to William Keith of Delny; and in 1591 George, Earl of Huntly, had the barony of Delny, including 'Tarrel'. Delny is only some dozen miles from Rockfield, whereas it is double that to the other Tarradale, in Urray; so it seems likely that this was the property referred to. In 1595, George Munro had the property of Tarrel, but this may have been *Meikle* Tarrel. He was a member of the Scots Parliament from 1617-21. Despite the inference of Meikle and Little, in an early 19th-century gazeteer, Little Tarrel is described as one of the two chief mansions of Tain parish—not Tarbet parish, as now—whereas the farm of Meikle Tarrel was not mentioned.

# TULLOCH CASTLE

Less than a mile north of the county town of Dingwall, Tulloch Castle stands within its policies on the south side of Tulloch Hill overlooking the Cromarty Firth. The present great house, now used for scholastic purposes, has been added to and altered at various periods. But the nucleus is a square, sturdy and fairly simple keep, probably of the early 16th century, with a circular stair-tower rising at its north-west angle. The parapet and corbelling of this keep are modern, as is the 'castellated' caphouse which tops the stair-tower and gives access to the flat roof. It seems likely that originally there would be the usual gabled garret storey within the parapet-walk, and the height of the caphouse supports this presumption. A number of the keep windows have been enlarged, but those of the stair-tower are original and small. The slit windows of the ground floor are likewise original, as are the gunloops, some of which have been built up. The basement course is massive and the walls are harled. An interesting feature is the way the south-west angle of the keep is chamfered off up to first-floor level, with a large shot-hole penetrating this chamfer from the basement.

There has been a large gabled addition to east and north, probably of the 17th century, and considerable later work and refacing here and elsewhere.

Internally many features of interest survive. The basement of the keep consists of vaulted cellars, in which the numerous gun-loop apertures are very evident. The Hall on the first floor has been remodelled and its windows enlarged, but the great fireplace remains, The first-floor apartments of the early additions still retain their fine ornamental plaster ceilings. That in the east wing is most handsome, with excellent pine panelling, and fine painted murals.

Tulloch was a barony of a family called Bain for many generations until in 1760 it passed to the Davidsons whose seat it was until recent times. Nearby is the Moot Hill, where the Bains dispensed justice within their jurisdiction, and there is a Gallows Hill conveniently close, with a cottage alleged to be that of the hangman of the barony of Tulloch.

[166]

# SHETLAND

## MUNESS CASTLE

Situated at the foot of the island of Unst, Muness has the distinction of being the most northerly fortalice in Britain. It is ruinous but more or less complete to the wallhead, a Z-planned structure of the late 16th-century, with a number of interesting features. The long main block lies approximately east and west, with round towers projecting to the north-west and south-east, and angle-turrets corbelled out at the other two corners. There have been two main storeys and an attic. The walls are of coursed rubble which has been harled, with freestone dressings. A feature is the variety and design of the many gunloops and shot-holes—wide-splayed, cross-shaped, quatrefoil, eliptical and round. The corbelling of the turrets is handsome, chequered above and continuous below. The windows are fairly small, with chamfered edges.

The door lies towards the east end of the south front, and is surmounted by decorative panels. The lower bears the quaint inscription: LIST ZE TO KNAW YIS BULDING QUHA BEGAN: LAURENCE THE BRUCE HE WAS THAT WORTHY MAN: QUHA ERNESTLY HIS AIRIS AND OFFSPRING PRAYIS: TO HELP AND NOT TO HURT THIS VARK ALUAYIS. THE ZEIR OF GOD 1598. Above a moulded heraldic panel, much weatherworn, bears the arms of Bruce and a lion rampant, with the initials L.B.

The entrance admits to a long vaulted passage from which are reached the kitchen at the far west end, with a chamber in the round tower off it, and three cellars, all vaulted. Another tower chamber opens off that to the east, which has been the wine-cellar, having the usual private stair to the Hall above. These two tower chambers have domed vaults. The kitchen has a wide fireplace, not in the gable but in the inner wall, which is unusual, and there is a stone sink and drain.

At the east end of the entrance corridor a straight scale stair rises, not a turnpike. The first floor contains the Hall at its centre

with smaller rooms to right and left in the main block and little circular chambers in the towers. The Hall has a fireplace, three windows and a number of aumbries. The west room has a fireplace, only one window, and a private turnpike stairway as the only access to the room directly above. The tower-room has only shot-hole lights. The east room is much intruded upon by the main and wine-cellar stair-wells and gives access to an octagonal room in the other tower, which in this case has a small fireplace and three windows. The upper floor is now ruinous but has contained a further three bedrooms. The angle-turrets were entered from this level.

There is now no sign of the former courtyard.

The castle was built, as indicated, by Laurence Bruce of Cultmalindie, Perthshire, whose wife was Elizabeth Gray, daughter of Patrick, 4th Lord Gray, and therefore aunt of the infamous Master of Gray. It may be only a coincidence that the Master's wife was the Lady Marie Stewart, daughter of Robert, Earl of Orkney, Mary Queen of Scots' half-brother, whose son, the notorious Earl Patrick, was at the same time building Scalloway Castle and the Earl's Palace, Kirkwall; apparently Laurence did not live to complete his castle, and perhaps obedient to the quoted inscription over the door, it was finished by his second son Andrew, whose initials were said formerly to have been visible below the south-west turret. And that Laurence Bruce's own mother had an illegitimate son by James the Fifth, who was the same Earl Robert. And that after committing murder in Perthshire Laurence fled North to his kinsman's remote Shetland property, to settle down at Muness.

# SCALLOWAY CASTLE

This well-known castle stands within the village of the same name, on the mainland of Shetland, formerly a burgh and the ancient capital. The fortalice was built in 1600 by the tyrannical Earl Patrick Stewart, nephew of Mary Queen of Scots, who compelled the local inhabitants to erect the building for him, without payment, on pain of forfeiting their properties. It is a fine house, nevertheless, L-planned and rising to four storeys and a garret. The walls are of coursed rubble with freestone dressings, harled, and though long roofless they remain entire to the wallhead. The main block lies east and west, with the wing extending southwards at the west end. A tall stair-turret projects at the north-east angle, and there is another, smaller, within the north-west re-entrant. Ordinary angle-turrets crown the other corners, and a notably tall chimney-stack, carrying the Hall flue, soars above the south wallhead. There are many shot-holes, round and quatrefoil.

The door is in the south-east re-entrant angle, in the wing, enhanced by no fewer than four decorative panels, much weather-worn, but one probably representing the royal arms. There were the usual two doors, of iron and wood, the bar-hole for which remains. These opened on to the main stair-foot, a wide scale-and-platt. To the left is a vaulted porter's lodge, and another small vault is contrived beneath the stairway, possibly a pit or prison. To the right of the door a vaulted passage runs the length of the main block, giving access to the two main ground-floor apart-

ments, that to the west being the kitchen, with a wide fireplace in the gable and a well opposite. The Hall occupies the entire first floor of the main block, a handsome chamber measuring 46 by 22 feet, with nine windows and two fireplaces set opposite each other. From the Hall are entered the two turret stairs to east and west, from which the upper storeys are reached. The second floor of the main block contained two good rooms, and the third three, all with fireplaces and some with garderobes. From these the angle-turrets were reached. In the wing there was a single room on each of the upper floors.

The castle makes a pleasing picture, whatever the hatred connected with its building and the harsh overlordship of these Stewarts. Earl Patrick, though a tyrant, did provide much of the islands' best domestic architecture, here and at the Earl's Palace in Kirkwall before ending his savage career on the executioner's block at Edinburgh in 1615.

# SUTHERLAND

## BALNAKEIL HOUSE

Superbly situated on a mound above a delightful sandy bay at
Durness, within a few miles of Cape Wrath, this is the old laird's
house of the great Durness estate, and the most north-westerly
example in Scotland. Originally Church lands, Balnakeil was a
residence of the Bishops of Caithness. There may be a nucleus
of this period still remaining, but basically the house appears to
belong to the 17th century, altered and extended the following
century. On a rocky and uneven site, it now follows the E-plan,
with a main block lying north and south and wings projecting
westwards at either end. A peculiar small square tower projects
westwards from the south end of the main block, looking as
though it should be a stair-tower—but there is no sign that it has
been so. Above a tiny vaulted basement it contains a small chamber on each floor, lit by a little window. There is a curious pro-

jection corbelled out in the re-entrant angle above first-floor level, the purpose of which is a mystery. It looks like the outward projection of a very small turret-stair, but internally it contains merely a long, high recess.

The oldest part of the house is said to be the northern wing, but the walling is very thick in various other portions. The walls are harled, and rise to three storeys and a garret, with the gables crowstepped. There is a tall chimneystack rising near the centre of the west wallhead, for the Hall fireplace. Most of the windows are very small, with chamfered edges. If there are any shot-holes, they are covered over by the harling.

There is a most unusual arrangement of vaulting in the basement of the north wing. The most easterly ground-floor chamber is the old kitchen, with a built-up arched fireplace in the east gable. Another vaulted cellar, at a somewhat lower level, occupies the north-west corner of wing and main block. But between these two, there is yet another vault, at a considerably lower level still, reached by a steep straight stair. This is almost like a pit, but appears to have had two exit doors, now built up.

There are two stairways in the house, neither of very early date. That in the north wing appears to date from the late 17th century, and is squared. On the first floor of the main block is the Hall, with a moulded stone fireplace. To the north is a handsome smaller room, panelled in pine.

By 1611, Balnakeil had passed to the Mackay family—this of course being their clan territory—a document of that date referring to William Mackay of Balnakeil. It later came into the hands of the chiefs of the clan, the Lords Reay, though there was some dispute about ownership with the Earls of Sutherland, which was finally settled in 1633. It is interesting to note that in the little ruined church close by, is a stone slab marking the interment of a notorious individual who was a relation of the Reay chief and in fact his paid murderer. The position of the slab on a side wall is said to indicate that, however, feared in his lifetime, it was considered doubtful whether this character should actually be buried in the church—as presumably his late employer desired. So he was interred in this position, under the walling, half-in, half-out of the holy building. The slab is highly decorative, showing a figure with bow-and-arrow shooting at a stag, above a heraldic panel and various initials. The lettering is somewhat weatherworn but seems to declare DONALD MAKMURCHOR HEIR LYIS LOW. VASIL (was ill) TO HIS FREIND, VAR TO HIS FOE, TRUE TO HIS MAISTER IN VERD AND VO 1623.

[172]

# DORNOCH CASTLE

Rising impressively and, with the cathedral across the street, dominating the little capital-town of Sutherland at the mouth of the Dornoch Firth, this tall and massive tower was the seat of the Bishops of Caithness—and by its character indicates that these prelates required to be strong in more than spiritualities. The building belongs to three main periods, the keep, the major portion of which is of early date; the late 16th-century alterations and additions thereto; and the large extensions of the early 19th century.

The keep is a lofty five storeys, with a circular stair-tower added at the south-east angle in the 16th century, this finishing in a conical roof and being enhanced by stringcourses. Its other angles are finished with typical 16th-century open rounds, and the gabled roof ornamented with crowsteps in the ecclesiastical style. Many of the windows have been enlarged, and some surmounted by relieving arches. The tower is defended by crosslet slits and shot-holes. A moulded 16th-century doorway opens in the base of the stair-tower. The wing to the east, partly 16th-century and partly later, is a storey lower, and notable for the enormous kitchen chimney-stack which dominates the east end of the south front. A secondary stair-tower, of ashlar, projects on the north front, rising from a squared base, and nearby is a

picturesque buttress. A courtyard has extended to west and south, the arched gateway of which survives. The main entrance to the tower is at first-floor level on the south front, the original access to which would be by a removable timber stair.

The building has had a chequered history, having been a bishop's palace, long a ruin, a courthouse and gaol, then the county buildings, and now is used as a hotel. The internal accommodation therefore has undergone considerable alteration and adaption. But the usual original arrangement of vaulted basement, Hall on first floor and sleeping accommodation higher, would prevail.

Just when the oldest part of the castle was built is not clear—although the cathedral across the road dates from 1245, when it was erected by the patriot Bishop Gilbert Murray. In 1567, George the turbulent 4th Earl of Caithness claimed the wardship of the young Earl of Sutherland, then a minor. This was contested by the local people—although Caithness was apparently supported by the nearby Sutherland of Skelbo, Lord of Duffus. The Master of Caithness, aided by Skelbo and Hugh Mackay of Strathnaver, then attacked and burned the town and cathedral of Dornoch, but the castle itself managed to hold out against this force for a month. The defenders eventually capitulated on terms and the provision of three hostages—who were treacherouly murdered. The castle was then burned, and remained in a ruinous state until 1814, when it was restored for municipal purposes.

# DUNROBIN CASTLE

Famous for centuries as the principal seat of the great Sutherland family, Dunrobin, sited commandingly on a height above the narrow coastal plain a mile or so north-east of Golspie, at first glance looks to be an enormous 'sham castle' of the Rhineland. But closer inspection reveals that its nucleus, in the north-east angle, is a quite large 17th-century mansion of traditional Scots construction, with the usual stair-towers, corbelling and crow-stepped gables. Inspect still further and it is discovered that this again is only an extension of a still earlier nucleus, an ancient square keep, with walls over 6 feet thick, finishing in a parapet and walk with open rounds—this last being now wholly surrounded by later work. This early tower is said to date from 1401, in which case it is by no means the original stronghold, for the family was based here before the 12th century. It is vaulted on each floor, an early feature, and its iron yett is still preserved. The large 17th-century mansion was added to south and west round a courtyard measuring 50 by 25 feet, and is on an E-shaped plan of three storeys and a garret, with slender stair-towers at the outer angles, that to the south apparently having been somewhat heightened. Another and larger circular stair-tower connects this work with the old keep, and this has pedimented windows bearing the initials of John, 14th Earl of Sutherland and his Countess. The walls are harled. The later additions were erected in 1785 and 1851.

Descended from the famous Freskin of Moravia, Hugh Freskin got a grant of territory in Sutherland from William the Lyon and came north to found this family. A descendant was created Earl of Sutherland in 1235. Although not of Celtic origin, they adopted the Gaelic style, and their chief became known as The Great Cat, adopting the cat as crest, allegedly on account of the prevalence of wild-cats in these parts—the origin of the name of Caithness, or Cattu-ness. The line persisted, playing a major role in Scots history for three hundred years, until it ended in an heiress, who married the second son of the 2nd Earl of Huntly, and so carried the Sutherland earldom to the Gordons. For the next two centuries the earls bore that name. Her grandson was forfeited for his share in Huntly's rebellion of 1562, and was exiled in Flanders. He came home five years later, however—but was poisoned at Helmsdale Castle by Isobel Sinclair, wife of his uncle, Gordon of Gartay, his wife with him. Their only son survived,

however, but was seized at Skibo Castle by the Sinclair Earl of Caithness, still a child, and forced to marry that earl's daughter, the profligate Lady Barbara Sinclair, twice his age, Caithness meantime taking up residence at Dunrobin. However, on attaining his majority he managed to divorce the lady, and married instead the Lady Jean Gordon, whom Bothwell had just divorced in order to marry Mary Queen of Scots. Their son was the 13th earl, whose son built the 17th-century extensions. He was much involved in the religious wars, opposed Montrose in his campaigns, and with 1,000 men arrived just too late to take part in the Battle of Dunbar against Cromwell. The 18th earl died young in 1766 leaving only a year-old daughter, the greatest landowner in Britain. She it was who later married the Marquis of Stafford, and they were created Duke and Duchess of Sutherland—the instigators of the notorious Sutherland Clearances.

Today, although still in the possession of a Countess of Sutherland in her own right, Dunrobin is used as a school.

# SKELBO CASTLE

The gaunt and battered remains of the ancient and powerful stronghold of the Sutherlands, Lords of Duffus, stands on a defensive rocky site above the south shore of the tidal Loch Fleet, four miles north of Dornoch. There is however an early 17th-century house still standing within the broken curtain-walling of the old castle, and although this is in a bad state of repair, the proprietor is at least considering restoration.

Dating from so much later than the rest of the castle—which may be of the 14th century—and on a lower level of the uneven site, this building would seem to have been a more or less new construction, erected against the old curtain-wall, rather than merely a wing added or altered. It is a lengthy oblong block of two storeys and a garret, lying approximately north and south, containing a range of vaulted cellars in the basement. The first floor now contains only the one large chamber, though it probably was subdivided originally, and the garret floor above has gone. There are signs that there may have been further building to the south. The masonry is of rough red sandstone rubble.

The building has obviously been greatly altered and adapted at various periods, most of the windows having been enlarged or built up, with new doorways opened. But certain original features remain. The arched doorway towards the north end still retains

its slot for a massive door-bar. A relieving arch surmounts the
window immediately to the south, and a small loophole window
survives between the doors at the south end. The walling is topped
by an eaves course, and the north-eastern skewputt is decorated
by a carved mask. Internally, little of interest remains, but there
has been a large arched fireplace in the north gable, presumably
the kitchen.

The Sutherlands of Skelbo were a branch of the same family
as the Earls of Sutherland, who likewise sprang from the famous
Freskin de Moravia, founder of the Moray or Murray family.
They seem to have gravitated north from Moray at an early date,
no doubt marrying heiresses. The Skelbo line, however, in due
course went back, or at least re-established contact with Moray,
for they inherited the great lordship of Duffus in the 14th century.
They seem to have continued to make Skelbo their main domicile,
however—and a turbulent line they were. William Sutherland,
Lord of Duffus, was killed by Clan Gunn, at Thurso, in 1530,
in a squabble over the Bishopric of Caithness, and his son and
heir was thrown into prison by the Privy Council for the scale of
his reprisals. *His* son, Alexander, attacked and sacked the nearby
town of Dornoch in 1567, and again in 1570. Oddly enough, we
read that the next year, having put to death certain sureties who
had surrendered to his ally the Earl of Caithness, he became over-
come with remorse and pined away to his grave. The laird who
succeeded in 1616 was rash enough to carry off the tiend-sheaves
already paid to the young Earl of Sutherland, depositing them in
his own barns at Skelbo, until forced by the Sheriff to disgorge.
The part of the castle with which we are concerned seems to have
been built by the son of this laird, created a peer by Charles the
First.

# MISCELLANEOUS

## BEDLORMIE HOUSE, WEST LOTHIAN

Standing on rising ground at the extreme western boundary of West Lothian, near the A89 road four miles west of Armadale, the ancient estate of Bedlormie, formerly Badlormie or Balormie, was for long a part of the barony of Ogilface. Originally its fortalice was a plain peel-type tower, square and vaulted; but the present building is a fairly typical L-shaped laird's house of the early 17th century, unfortunately lowered in height by a storey and otherwise altered. It is now a whitewashed farmhouse.

The main block lies east and west, with the wing projecting northwards, and in the re-entrant angle rises a circular stair-tower with conical roof—now, because of the lowering of the general roof-level, looking somewhat out-of-proportion. The crow-stepped gables have gone, of course, and the only external features remaining are the roll-mouldings of the ground-floor win-

[179]

dows. One, facing north in the main block, appears to have borne an inscribed lintel, but this is now too weatherworn to be decipherable. On the south front, near the present doorway, is a very small moulded light. The upper windows are of later date, larger and having chamfered margins. The original doorway, presumably, would be near the stair-tower in the re-entrant. The interior, which is not vaulted in the basement, has been completely modernised, the only remaining feature of interest being the fairly wide turnpike stairway.

As early as 1424 the Register of the Great Seal records Sir John Murray of Ogilface granting the lands of Bedlormie to Sir John Forrester of Corstorphine. This appears to have been only a temporary alienation, however—although the Forresters appear again later in Bedlormie's history—for the Ogilface barony had passed to the increasingly powerful West Lothian family of Livingstone, Lords Livingstone of Callendar and Earls of Linlithgow, by the 16th century, Bedlormie with it. In 1563 James Livingstone of Bedlormie was laird, though a family named Walker appear in various local records as tenants. In 1607 the Ogilface barony was held by Alexander Livingstone, Earl of Linlithgow, and he made temporary grant of Bedlormie to George Forrester, possibly his nephew, son and heir of Sir Henry Forrester of Corstorphine and his wife Cristine Livingstone. The lands returned to the Livingstones however, and became settled in a cadet branch of the house, which in time rose to the dignity of baronets. The last of this family, indeed the last representer of the male line of the Earls of Linlithgow, was Sir Thomas Livingstone of Bedlormie and Westquarter, who was also the last Keeper of the Palace of Linlithgow, and who died in 1853, when the titles became extinct.


## BRUNSTANE HOUSE, EDINBURGH

Here is a large and substantial mansion, on the face of it dating from the late 17th century, situated in a corner of green country still remaining behind the Edinburgh suburb of Joppa, tall, typical and symmetrical, and with a history fairly well-known and documented. Yet it is not quite what it seems. For it is far from homogeneous, and the tracing of its components is much less simple than might be expected. Since 1673 it has been a large E-shaped edifice of three storeys and a garret, the main block lying roughly east and west, with wings projecting northwards and semi-octagonal stair-towers rising in the two re-entrants, one with a conical

and the other an ogee roof, and square towers with hipped roofs projecting from the opposite, outer, angles. Nevertheless, it dates from at least four periods. There was a nucleus, probably a simple square tower, which was destroyed after the Battle of Pinkie in 1547, fought nearby, and the very massive 8-feet thick gable-end of the north-east wing probably represents part of this fortalice. This was rebuilt and added to, in the same century, probably to form a typical L-shaped tower-house, and in the main this is represented by the south-east angle of the building, although there are a number of internal features here which are difficult to explain. Then, in 1639, this L-shaped house was again altered, extended and given a wide stair-tower in the re-entrant, plus the projecting square tower to the back, or south-east, by John Maitland, Earl and first Duke of Lauderdale, the 'uncrowned King of Scotland'. Some thirty years later, the same man, at the height of his power, employed the famous King's Architect, Sir William Bruce, to double the size of the house by adding a duplicate extension, another L, to the west, this time giving the stair and square towers ogee roofs. Apart from a single-storey frontal corridor, almost an elongated porch, along the courtyard front, added by the 18th-century judge Lord Milton, Brunstane has remained unchanged since then. The two main portions, however, are now occupied as two distinct dwellings, of which only that to the east, the earlier portion, falls within the scope of this book. It is interesting to note, however, although confusing, that beneath the western range are deep underground cellars, giving an impression of much earlier work than 1673.

Masked by the porch, the eastern house is entered by a hand-somely moulded doorway in the foot of the stair-tower, surmounted by a heraldic panel, with the Earl of Lauderdale's arms, dated 1639. The stairway is a wide turnpike, giving access to all floors. The ground floor is not now vaulted, although the ceiling of the old kitchen, the north-easterly chamber, is most curiously finished in a 'rib-and-fluting' fashion unique in my experience. In the very thick gable was the arched fireplace, 12 feet wide, and at the east side of this is a deep wall-chamber, somewhat rounded internally, which may have represented the well of a stairway in the early tower. There are traces of small windows externally.

An interesting feature of the external walling at the south-east angle, is the curious corbelled-out projection, of no great thickness, at first-floor level, for purposes unknown, which is interrupted by the square projecting tower, indicating that this was part of the late 16th-century development. Another puzzle in a house notable for such, is the presence of two thick internal walls in the eastern wing, much thicker than the lateral walls, only a room apart, both of which give the impression of having been outer walls. At garret level, a doorway in one of these has been slapped through a chimney-flue, the vent for which is still open above. Also at this level, in the northern gable, are two small openings, now built up, flanking the fireplace, splayed internally like shot-holes.

There are many interesting features throughout the house, in mouldings and plasterwork, but mainly dating from the later periods of reconstruction and redecoration, and some good pine panelling.

The career of John Maitland, Duke of Lauderdale, is too well-known to require mention here. His first wife was a daughter of the first Earl of Home, and her arms are displayed with his own over the 1639 doorway. He married, secondly, the notorious Elizabeth Murray, Countess of Dysart, thought to have been the mistress of Oliver Cromwell—as well as of others.

## CAERLAVEROCK CASTLE, DUMFRIESSHIRE

There tends to be some confusion about the dating of this famous castle, so prominent in Scotland's story. In woodland to the south of the present building are the inconspicuous foundations of an earlier stronghold. The present splendid red-stone facade, dates in fact only from the early 15th century, although incorporating

earlier work also. Additions later in that century and in the two following, complicate the description.

The style is unusual in Scotland, built on a triangular plan with massive twin drum-towers and backing keep or gatehouse at the apex, and circular flanking-towers at the other two angles, that to the south-west remaining entire. High curtain-walls, crowned formerly by parapet-walks, link these towers and enclose a court-yard, against which subsidiary buildings have been erected at various periods, while a tall and handsome 'palace' block was added at the east side in the early 17th century. The whole establishment is islanded by a wide moat, beyond which have been earthworks and outer ditches. Little of the south range, wherein has been a magnificent Hall, and other features, remains; but elsewhere the building is, at least externally, mainly entire to the wallhead.

The entrance is by an arched and recessed gateway between the drum-towers, formerly approached by a drawbridge, with port-cullis, and surmounted by a much weatherworn heraldic panel with the Maxwell arms. The gateway was further defended by great draw-bars, and flanked by numerous wide gunloops; while above were the usual corbelled machicolations for hurling down missiles. The entrance pend leads through to the courtyard, with guard-rooms on either side, from which are reached the basement-chambers of the drum-towers, all these apartments being vaulted. The drum-towers are four storeys high, with their attic floors above now gone. This unusual keep-plus-drum-towers complex is surmounted by a ruinous square caphouse, with angle-turrets, of the 16th century, and the whole has had a wide parapet-walk, the massive corbel-course for which is a prominent feature.

[183]

To give any detailed description of this great castle internally is beyond the scope of this work. Each of the upper floors of the keep formerly contained one large apartment, reached by a small turnpike stair in the south-west angle; but these were subdivided in the 16th century and extra fireplaces added, with two larger wheel-stairs. The round flanking-tower to the south-west was called Murdoch's Tower, commemorating the imprisonment therein of Murdoch, Duke of Albany, the King's ambitious cousin, before his execution in 1425 by James the First. It is four storeys high, of the same period but smaller than the drum-towers, with a postern gate and access to the curtain-wall-walk. The splendid 'palace' block is highly decorative in Renaissance style, three storeys and an attic, its decorative door and window architraves being notable. Internally this building contained excellent domestic offices in the vaulted basement—kitchen, servery, well-chamber and bakery—with large public apartments above having fine fireplaces and accessories, and many bedrooms higher.

The building, after being long a neglected ruin, is now well cared for by the Ministry of Works, and deservedly popular with visitors.

Caerlaverock, of course, was the main seat and home of the powerful family of Maxwell. Sir Eustace Maxwell was keeper during the Wars of Independence, after Edward the First's famous siege. He threw in his lot belatedly with Bruce only two years before Bannockburn; but Bruce recognised the danger of strong castles and had Caerlaverock demolished. It was rebuilt, and in 1347 Sir Eustace's son, Herbert, changed allegiance once more, to the English cause. Ten years afterwards the Scots again took the castle, and dismantled it. By 1425 however, the Maxwells were securely back, and from this period and onwards date practically all that we see today. Impossible here to even hint at the stirring history of this noble pile, until in 1640 it held out for King Charles for 13 weeks against the Commonwealth forces, under another Maxwell, Robert, first Earl of Nithsdale, and was thereafter finally deserted.

## CAVERS HOUSE, ROXBURGHSHIRE

This tall gaunt shell of the former great castle of Cavers stands amongst green knowes on high ground some three miles east of Hawick, above the valley of the Teviot, in a reduced estate still owned by the descendants of the notable line of Douglas of Cavers,

[184]

Hereditary Sheriffs of Teviotdale. A large and composite mansion, much of it modern, was entire and in occupation until recent times, when the present proprietor demolished the modern building and removed the roof and much else from the keep. However, sufficient of the latter remains to give a fair indication of its original appearance, especially from the southern aspect, although a number of 'castellated' features surviving are in fact modern.

It is a massive and lofty tower-house of five storeys and an attic, oblong on plan, with a flush parapet and walk along the south side only, with crowstepped gables east and west. The masonry of the immensely thick walling is ashlar up to third-floor level, with good coursed rubble above of later date. A modern panel at third-floor level on the east face, and dated 1200, appears to refer to the lower work, which certainly is of early date. The upper parts, before modernisation, probably were of 16th-century construction. Most of the windows have been enlarged, but some of the lower lights into the basement, are small and original. A piscina, somewhat defaced, remains on the south wall at first-floor level. No internal features have been left. The position has been a fairly strong one, with the ground falling away sharply to south and east. There was probably a moat or ditch to west and north, approachable by a draw-bridge.

Cavers was originally a seat of the Baliol family in the 12th and

13th centuries, and as such was held by the English and Baliol-Comyn interest against Bruce during the Wars of Independence, as late as 1313. On the triumph of Bruce, the house of Douglas which had supported him of course, rose high, the Good Sir James being probably his closest friend and collaborator. The oldest portion of the present building is thought to have been built by Sir Archibald Douglas, younger son of the famous 2nd Earl of Douglas who, dying, won the Battle of Otterburn—who was the son of Good Sir James's nephew. The Douglases of Cavers played a very prominent part in Scotland's history over the centuries, not all of it on the side of the Crown; and no attempt can be made here to chronicle it. The direct male line failed with James Douglas, 20th laird, when the property passed to his niece, who married a Captain Edward Palmer in 1879. The Palmer-Douglas line continues.

## CRAIGMILLAR CASTLE, EDINBURGH

One of the best-known landmarks of Edinburgh, this great castle crowns a green ridge three miles south of the city, above its spreading modern housing. Although it looks a complicated and mighty fortress, in fact it is a fairly simple composition, stemming from a massive plain late 14th-century L-planned tower, extended by the addition of lofty parapeted curtain-walls with circular angle-towers a century later; and a further large walled enclosure, within a moat, plus lean-to buildings, and a chapel, within the courtyards, in the 16th century. The building, though roofless, is well maintained.

The original tower rises to four main storeys, with its wing a storey higher and finishing in a 16th-century gabled watch-chamber. A flush parapet surmounts the main block wallhead, with wide and shallow crenellations. The entrance is by a wide arched doorway in the wing, under a heraldic panel of the Preston family. It opens into a narrow vaulted lobby which leads to the turnpike stair and also gives access to the main block basement, subdivided and dimly-lit cellars. These each now have doorways slapped through the 10-foot thick walls to east and west, linking with later work. There is an entresol floor above, of timber, and above this the main vaulted ceiling, the lobbies also being vaulted. Another small turnpike rises to the main first floor. Here is the Hall, a fine apartment of 35 by 21 feet, with a vaulted chamber in the wing, now called Queen Mary's Room, but the original kitchen. The

Hall has a good hooded fireplace with a stone kerb, and the windows have stone seats. There are two garderobes. The kitchen had a wide arched fireplace with stone sink and slop.

Still another small turnpike leads to the main second floor, another vaulted entresol. The large chamber has no fireplace, but the vaulted apartment in the wing has, also a garderobe with chute. Above this level is the low-pitched, stone-slabbed roof of the main block, within the parapet-walk; also the gabled watch-chamber, with its own fireplace and garderobe, which also serves as caphouse for the stairhead.

The 30-foot high curtain-walls are very fine, with a good parapet-walk carried on heavy machicolated corbelling. The angle-towers also have machicolated parapets. There is a large square corbelled projection at the south wallhead, adjoining the keep. Westwards the wallhead has lost its crenellations and parapet, and there are socket-holes for a timber gallery or bretache.

The later buildings within the courtyard comprise a four-storey range on the east, containing four cellars, three vaulted, in basement, reached by a vaulted passage from the keep. These included a well-chamber, later kitchen, and a bakehouse with a round oven and stone table. The floor above also has four apartments, two vaulted, reached by a large turnpike stair contrived partly in the keep's walling. The middle chamber is still another kitchen, with huge fireplace, for which the massive chimney-stack seen in sketch houses the flue. Above was a single long apartment, communicating with the parapet-walk, no doubt a dormitory for the guard.

The west range of outbuildings dates from 1661, although there is an older nucleus of vaulted cellarage. Otherwise each storey contains three chambers, the central one long and narrow. In the outer court the chapel has been fairly plain. It dates from the mid-16th century, with crowstepped gables, and has a screen and piscina. The round flanking-tower, with gunloops, at the extreme north-east angle of the outer curtain, was a dovecote.

There are a number of heraldic panels, dates and carved initials, of the Preston and Gilmour families, and others. Sir Simon Preston of Gorton purchased Craigmillar in 1374 from John de Capella, and the family retained possession for nearly three centuries. The castle was notable for the use made of it by Scots royalty. James the Third imprisoned his brother, the Earl of Mar here. The young James the Fifth, with his tutor Gavin Douglas, was sent here to escape the plague raging in Edinburgh. Mary Queen of Scots so often made the Prestons' castle a residence that the nearby hamlet where her French ladies were installed got the name of Little France. At the so-called Conference of Craigmillar, Moray, Lethington, Bothwell and others proposed the Queen's divorce from Darnley. And here her son, James the Sixth, planned his famous excursion to Denmark to fetch his bride. In 1660 the castle was sold to Sir John Gilmour, Lord President, and the castle remained with his descendants.

## CRICHTON CASTLE, MIDLOTHIAN

This historic castle stands attractively on the lip of the picturesque valley of the Tyne, ten miles from Edinburgh and two south-west of Path-head. Long ruinous, it remains fairly intact to the wallhead, after considerable early alteration, and is now in the care of the Ministry of Works.

The building belongs to four main periods—the 14th-century tower-house from which all sprang; large 15th-century extensions within the original courtyard; and a small but elaborate late 16th-century wing to the north-east, with notable decorative work of the later period, when this was the seat of the notorious and extravagant Francis Stewart, 4th Earl of Bothwell.

The simple keep, built of excellent squared ashlar 7 feet thick, is in the centre of the north front, beside the present entrance. It rises to only three storeys, having lost its top probably at the time of the first extensions. The basement is vaulted and has the usual wooden loft as entresol. The Hall on the first floor is also vaulted,

and 24 feet high, with a wide moulded fireplace, and a screened-off area to the north-east as very modest kitchen. Below this is a most unpleasant mural pit or prison, known as the Massie More, only 7 by 6½ feet, with its door 2½ feet high, and a tiny slit for air.

The first addition lies to the south of the keep, the work of Sir William Crichton, famous Chancellor of Scotland in the mid-15th century. Oblong and of three storeys, it would have a garret storey above the handsome machicolated individual corbels for the support of the parapet. A slightly projecting tower rises at the south-east angle, to house a small turnpike stair. In the re-entrant of this is a small and picturesque angle-turret to guard the present door, of later date. This range was built as a gatehouse-tower, with a central arched entrance, now built up. The basement contained the entrance pend, with vaulted cellars on either side. On the first floor was another large hall, later subdivided, with enriched stonework and a large hooded fireplace. Also a pantry and buttery to the west. Above was yet another hall, with fine stone cornice.

In the second half of the same century another large addition was made to the west (as seen in sketch). At the south-west angle this was built up to form a tall parapeted tower. The external windows here are notably small, and there is a small postern towards the north end. The basement is vaulted, save, strangely, for the tower-foot. Here is another range of kitchen and public rooms on the first floor, with bedrooms higher.

The last and north wing, though in its base another 15th-century extension is in the main dating from 1581-91, its upper works of gables, angle-turrets, chimney-copes, gunloops and continuous corbel-courses being typical of that period. It has a large and well-lit dining-room and withdrawing-room, over a range of vaulted cellars and a bakehouse, with much sleeping accommodation above. There is a remarkable portico to the courtyard and the Italianate workmanship of much of the wing is famous, particularly the diamond-panelled facade and pilasters. There is a deep draw-well in the piazza.

A building which looks like a chapel lies to the south. It was in fact stabling with accommodation for grooms.

With three of Scotland's most colourful and historical characters as owners—Chancellor Crichton; Mary Queen of Scots' Bothwell; and his nephew Francis Stewart, the bane of James the Sixth's life; it is possible only to hint at the exciting story of this splendid castle. The Crichtons were here in the 13th century, and the original tower was probably built by the Chancellor's father. The lands were forfeited in 1483, when the 3rd Lord supported Albany against James the Third, and given to one of the King's favourites, Sir John Ramsay, created Lord Bothwell, who turned English spy against James the Fourth. That king gave Crichton to Patrick Hepburn, Lord Hailes, created Earl of Bothwell, who left the castle for Flodden in 1514 and did not come home. The castle was besieged by the Protestant Lords in 1559. Mary Queen of Scots came here in 1562 for the wedding of one of her many illegitimate half-brothers, and is reputed to have spent part of her honeymoon with Darnley at Crichton. Her third husband's successor, the half-crazy Francis Stewart, however ungovernable, was a cultured ruffian, and having spent exiles in Italy, was responsible for much of the excellent architecture seen today.

## DENMILN CASTLE, FIFE

Standing at the roadside, in a farm-steading, one mile south-east of Newburgh, this is a rather unusual fortalice of the late 16th century, ruinous but with the main features surviving. Its cruciform plan is almost unique, with a main block lying approximately east and west, a squared stair-wing projecting centrally to the north, and opposite this a peculiar smaller rectangular tower, solid stone at the foot but on each of the upper floors housing a tiny lobby. This is used to enable access to be gained round the end of the central partition wall which divides each storey of the main block into two apartments, without the need for an intercommunicating door therein—a highly unusual arrangement. It seems hardly conceivable that the builders should have gone to the trouble of erecting this special tower for this purpose, and it may have originally had some other function, perhaps to house garderobes. Even so, it is a strange feature.

The castle contains three main storeys, with a garret floor above. A parapet and walk crowned the east gable only, supported on massive individual corbels of three members, with cannon-like spouts for draining the walk still projecting above. The windows are fairly large, and there are a number of wide splayed gunloops at basement level. The moulded entrance is in the re-entrant angle facing north-west, in the foot of the stair-wing, guarded by gun-loops. It opens on to the foot of a fairly wide turnpike. The basement contains two vaulted chambers, neither provided with the usual wide arched fireplace which represents the kitchen. Each of the upper rooms, two to each storey, has a fireplace; presumably the larger apartment at first-floor level was the Hall. There has been a courtyard to the west, and it seems probable that the kitchen premises were housed in a lean-to building therein. A dovecote to the south is dated 1706, with the initials of Sir Michael Balfour and his wife Dame Marjory Moncrieff.

In 1452 Denmylne was given to James Balfour, son of Sir John Balfour of Balgarvy, by James the Second for faithful service, and the family held the property until 1710. The burial aisle was in the old ruined St. Magridin's church at Abdie, near Lindores Loch, and memorials include one to Sir Michael, member of the royal household of Charles the Second who 'died of old age and disease 1652 in his 72nd year'; and his son Sir James, knight-baronet,

[191]

Lord Lyon King of Arms, well-known antiquary and friend of Drummond of Hawthornden, a 'student of the distant past accurate as he was eager, the darling and apple of the eye of the Muses', died 1657. A brother of this last was Sir Andrew Balfour, 1630-94, physician and founder of Edinburgh's first botanical garden.

## DOUNE CASTLE, PERTHSHIRE

This magnificent castle, one of the most famous in the land, was built at the end of the 14th and beginning of the 15th centuries, to succeed the stronghold on Inch Talla in the Lake of Menteith as the principal messuage-place of the great earldom of Menteith, or more properly Monteith. It stands in a strong site above the junction of the Ardoch Burn and the River Teith, just below the town of Doune. Although probably containing an older nucleus, most of the present building was erected by Robert, Duke of Albany—who married the Menteith heiress—and his son, Murdoch, both Regents during the long captivity of their kinsman James the First.

The castle consists of two great and tall keeps, linked by a lower range, to form the north side of a quadrangular courtyard, the other three sides being enclosed by a 40-foot-high curtain-wall, 8 feet thick, crowned by a parapet and walk, with open circular turrets at the angles and semi-circular bartisans corbelled out midway. Of the two keeps, that to the north-east is the larger and higher, a massive, roughly rectangular building of five main storeys and a garret, with a semi-circular tower projecting at the north-east angle. It is crowned by a flush parapet flanking a gabled roof to north and south only, the wall-walks of these connecting only by open flights of steps up and over the pitched roof at each end—a highly unusual arrangement. The stairhead rises to form a lofty look-out platform, reached from the eastern flight of steps. The north-west keep is somewhat lower, four storeys and a garret, but also having a flush parapet and gabled roof. There are a number of machicolated projections here, three grouped fairly close together, the largest above a built-up arched-headed postern gate to the west. The area between the two keeps is occupied by a long two-storeyed building. The courtyard is large and contains a deep draw-well.

The entrance is by an arched gateway in the main keep, admitting to a steeply-rising, cobbled and vaulted pend, with a

vaulted porter's lodge and inner chamber to one side, and a
guardroom and dark beehive-vaulted pit or prison to the other.
Elsewhere in the basement is a range of vaulted cellars and store-
houses, from certain of which narrow stairs in the walling mount
to the floor above. Indeed a feature of this castle is the large
number of unconnected narrow stairways. The main access to the
first floor is by two outside forestairs from the courtyard, one
leading to the lord's quarters, the other to the retainers'. The
Lord's Hall is a handsome vaulted apartment, with a splendid
double fireplace, and has been restored with modern panelling.
The banqueting and/or retainers' hall alongside occupies all the
lower wing at this level, an enormous chamber open to the rafters.
There is no normal fireplace here, but a central hearth has been
contrived, and if this was original then the smoke must have
found its way out of a hole in the roofing where there is now a
louvre. Particularly interesting are the kitchen premises in the
west tower, at this level, consisting of the kitchen itself, with an
enormous arched fireplace, area for an oven, and two slop-
drains; also a handsome 'arcaded' servery, of highly modern
aspect. Above this level were ample private and sleeping apartments in both towers.

The Doune of Menteith's history was inextricably linked with
that of the House of Stewart. From here Murdoch, Duke of

Albany, was summoned to imprisonment and then execution by the much-wronged James the First. Thereafter the castle merged with the Crown, until James the Fourth settled it on his Queen, Margaret Tudor, who in 1525 passed it to her third husband Henry Stewart, Lord Methven, a descendant of Albany. James the Fifth granted it to another of the same line, whose grandson became the Bonnie Earl of Moray through marriage with the Regent Moray's daughter. Since then the castle has remained with the Stewart Earls of Moray. Mary Queen of Scots resided here. It was garrisoned for Prince Charles Edward by a nephew of Rob Roy, and from its walls Home, the author of *Douglas*, escaped by means of a blanket-rope.

The building was restored in 1883, and is kept in good condition by the present Earl of Moray. It is a favourite venue for visitors.

## DOWIES HOUSE, WIGTOWNSHIRE

Remotely situated in the marshy valley of the Monreith Burn two miles north-east of Monreith village, Dowies is a most interesting fortified laird's house of mainly early 17th-century date, latterly used as a farmhouse but now derelict. It has a number of unusual features.

The plan is cross-shaped, the main block lying approximately east and west with a square wing projecting to the south and a circular stair-tower to the north. There are two storeys and an attic beneath a steep roof and no crowsteps to the gables. The windows are fairly small, many with simple roll mouldings. Above one on the first floor of the west gable is a projecting gargoyle mask. The two arrow-slit windows in the basement of the south wing are unexpected, giving an appearance of greater antiquity, and one has an ogival head. There are two good shot-holes at first- and second-floor level in the stair-tower. The door has been originally in the foot of this and is now reduced to a window, with some more elaborate moulding remaining. Above is an empty panel-space with a chequered surround. The present doorway to the south is modern. A tall and massive hall chimney-stack rises from eaves level to the west of the stair-tower. Unsightly outbuildings have been added to north and west.

Internally the building has been denuded of almost all interesting features, though the good turnpike stair remains and there are traces of the original panelling in window embrasures. There

has been no vaulting. There are two chambers on each floor in the main block, and a small apartment in the wing. The large hall fireplace on the first floor has been reduced.

This building could still be saved, and restored, would make an attractive residence.

Its history is interesting. Formerly named Moure, this was the original possession in Wigtownshire of the Maxwell family. Sir Edward Maxwell of Tinwald, second son of Herbert, 1st Lord Maxwell, acquired these lands in 1481, from a Cunninghame of Aikhead. Although there was an earlier castle nearby, the nucleus of the present building was occupied by his descendants until 1683, when they obtained the Tower of Myretoun nearby—still standing ruinous in the Monreith estate—from the McCullochs, and moved thereto. This building after a period of neglect, was somewhat altered, especially at the roofline, eventually becoming merely a farmhouse. Its site would be a strong one, for the now marshy valley was formerly a loch.

One of this family, John Maxwell of Garrerie, was convicted of the murder of John McKie of Glassoch and beheaded in 1619. The eldest son of a later laird, John Maxwell also, was a fervent Covenanter, and escaping at the Battle of Rullion Green, in Lothian rode home without stopping. His old father was so impressed by this, that he declared the horse had done enough in one day for a lifetime, and built a special stone-walled field for it, called the Horse Park, where the gallant steed spent the rest of its days—not entirely idly however, for under the name of Pentland, the stallion left a great many descendants of note in Galloway.

The property still belongs to the Maxwells of Monreith.

# EASTEND HOUSE, LANARKSHIRE

Set in a large wooded estate on the north-east flank of Tinto Hill, about two miles west of Thankerton, in Carmichael parish, this is a very ancient lairdship, and its house one that has grown through many generations of the same family. Although it is claimed to have a still earlier nucleus, the oldest evident part of the present building is a simple square keep, probably of the first half of the 16th century. To this has been added, at east and west, tall gabled wings, crowstepped and slender, dating from 1673. These in turn have been joined up, to the south, by a typical 18th-century bow-fronted addition, encasing the keep on that side. Finally, in the late 19th century, there have been large 'Scottish-Baronial' extensions to the west, less aggressively Victorian than is often the case, however, which blend fairly successfully with the whole.

The keep, of which only the north front and a little of the east side is left clear, has been very similar to a great many smallish fortalices of that period. Its walls, of good coursed rubble, harled, rise three storeys to a crenellated parapet borne on simple individual corbels, with open rounds at the angles, these on continuous corbelling. There is the usual gabled garret storey above, within the parapet-walk. The windows have been enlarged, save for one narrow slit. A stringcourse runs at first-floor level, and is continued round the 17th-century wing to the east.

It is impossible to give any description of the original internal arrangements, for the keep has been almost wholly gutted, partly

to provide space for the wide well of an 18th-century stairway to all floors. The only feature I discovered was a small slit window near the south-east corner at first-floor level, now built up in what is now an interior wall, which may have represented the position of the original turnpike stair. Even the basement vaulting has gone. The entrance to the keep used to be at the first floor, reached by the usual removable timber stair or gangway, and latterly given a stone forestair, now removed.

The Carmichaels of Eastend have been settled here from a very early period. Indeed some authorities reckon them to be senior to the chiefly family of Carmichael of Carmichael. In 1568 there was a marriage contract for Carmichael of Eastend; and in 1597 the laird was Michael Carmichael of Eastend. In the Privy Council records of 1609 we read that Thomas Carmichael of East-end, along with other followers of the Douglases, including other Carmichael and Lanarkshire lairds, were accused of bearing evil will against Andro, Lord Stewart of Ochiltree, on account of the slaughter of James, Lord Torthorwald; they were charged to appear before the Council to give assurances of keeping the King's peace, under pain of rebellion, and to find caution not to injure the person of the said Lord Ochiltree.


# ECCLESIAMAGIRDLE HOUSE, PERTHSHIRE

This attractive and typical small fortified laird's house of the early 17th century, takes its extraordinary name from a detached portion of Dron parish in lower Strathearn, the word, locally pronounced Ecclesmagriddle or Exmagriddle, meaning the Church of St. Grill, or Grillan. Until told of its existence by a friend, the author had never so much as heard of this house or seen any mention of the lairdship in all the research he has done—a highly unusual situation. Presumably the Lairds of Ecclesiamagirdle managed to keep notably well out of all recorded history, stirring events, lawsuits, marriage contracts and the like; and the house itself is unlikely to be discovered, situated as it is within the private estate of another and more modern mansionhouse known as Glenearn House, about two miles south-west of Bridge of Earn.

Delightfully sited in a woodland setting on the south shore of a small lochan, the building conforms to the T-plan, with a main block lying east and west and the stair-wing projecting centrally southwards. The walls rise to three storeys, with the stair-wing a storey higher, to contain the usual little watch-chamber, with

its own fireplace and chimney-stack, reached by a turret-stair corbelled out in the re-entrant angle, this turret having an over-sailing roof. The entrance is rather unusual in being in the foot of the stair-wing but on its south front, not in the re-entrant. The doorway has a roll-moulding and is surmounted by a heraldic panel. The long north face is entirely plain save for the dormer-windows. The ground floor is vaulted and would contain the kitchen, with the Hall on the first floor, with private room along-side, and bedroom accommodation higher.

There is additional building to the west, and there has been a courtyard to the south. This is entered by an arched gateway sur-mounted by a panel dated 1648, with the initials S.D.C. and D.A.C., for Sir David Carmichael of Balmedie and Dame Anne, his wife.

These lands were a property of the Abbey of Lindores as early as the 12th century. Saint Grill or Grillan is said to have been one of the twelve helpers who landed with Columba at Iona. His ancient small church was in a grove of yews nearby. In its grave-yard are two Covenanting memorials, one to Thomas Small who 'died for Religion, Covenant, King and Countrie 1st September 1645'.

At the Reformation period, the lands of Lindores Abbey were granted to Sir Patrick Leslie, a son of the 5th Earl of Rothes, who married one of the daughters of the Kings' illegitimate uncle, Robert Stewart, Earl of Orkney. He became Commendator of Lindores, and later Lord Lindores, and obtained Ecclesiamagirdle with the rest. He seems to have sold 'Eglismagirdill' to William Halyburton of Pitcur, and in 1629 King James confirmed a charter of the lands from Halyburton to David Carmichael of Balmedie, who presumably thereupon built the present house. One of the few references to Ecclesmagirdle appears in Macfarlane's *Geographical Collections*, of the date 1723. A rhyme, not very complimentary to the local beauties, runs thus:

> The lasses o' Exmagirdle may weel be dun,
> For frae Michaelmas to Whitsunday they never see the sun.

This, of course, refers to the situation of the place, nestling close under the northern slopes of the Ochils, denied the winter sun.

## EVELAW TOWER, BERWICKSHIRE

This interesting small fortalice, although ruinous, is still fairly entire to the wallhead, and appears to date from the 16th century. It is remotely situated on the high moorlands that form the southern flank of the Lammermuir Hills, overlooking the Merse three miles north-east of Westruther village and about a mile east of Wedderlie House. Farm-buildings adjoin and indeed abutt to the north, and screen that front and the re-entrant.

The building, three storeys and a garret in height, is L-shaped, and built of very rough grey rubble, with red sandstone dressings. The angles are rounded, but corbelled out to the square at eaves-level to facilitate the construction of the roof. There are wide splayed gunloops in the centres of the south and east fronts. The other fronts are either masked or have been altered.

The wing of the L, which forms a stair-tower, is unusual. This rises to a parapet carried on individual corbels, rounded at the angles, and the top storey is vaulted—a notable feature. The parapet itself has gone, but the head of the vault remains, grass-grown. Presumably there was a flat platform roof. The windows are very small, and mainly barred with iron—not grilles. The larger windows of the Hall have been filled in. A turret-stair has risen in the re-entrant angle above first-floor level, but only traces remain.

Internally the tower is completely ruinous. The entrance has been in the re-entrant, now covered by later lean-to building. The main block basement has been vaulted, and has contained the kitchen, with wide fireplace in the west gable. There has been a roomy turnpike stair to the first floor, which has contained the Hall, and above was sleeping accommodation reached by the narrow turret stair, An unusual feature is the manner in which

semi-circular alcoves have been contrived in two corners of the
Hall, and also above, utilising the curved angles of the outer
walling. It has been suggested that these contained small private
stairways, but they are too small for this, there are no sign of
treads, and three stairways rising from this level in such a small
tower is hardly conceivable.

Evelaw has proved very difficult to put into historical perspec-
tive. Only discovery that its ancient name was Ivelie, sometimes
spelt Yfle or Yiffle, enabled me to discover its background. It
originally belonged to the Abbey of Dryburgh, but in 1576, the
Commendator thereof confirmed its sale to William Douglas, in
Cockburnspath. The Douglases of Ivelie thereafter are occasion-
ally mentioned. In 1621 William Douglas of Ivelie ratified,
amongst others a Crown charter restoring his hereditary rights
to Francis Stewart, son of the infamous Francis Hepburn Stewart,
Earl of Bothwell, of James the Sixth's time, who had been so involved in the witchcraft activities. In 1634 the laird was Sir
Robert Douglas of Blackerston. His heiress carried the property
to Sir Robert Sinclair of Longformacus, who died 1678. A successor, Sir John, sold Ivelie in 1731 to a farm tenant named
Archibald Smith.


## OLD FAIRNILEE, SELKIRKSHIRE

Standing close to the modern mansion, in a wooded estate above
the Tweed some three miles north of Selkirk, this attractive little
tower is only part of a larger rectangular mansion, most of which

has gone. However, it is possible that what remains does represent the original house of the late 16th century, and the demolished portion was a 17th-century addition. McGibbon & Ross show the building as in 1887 and remark that there had been an attempt to build to a symmetrical design, with a central doorway and angle-turrets at each end. But their drawing shows differences in the corbelling of the turrets, and there are many more windows in the missing eastern portion. Also the dividing wall is very thick for an internal one, and might possibly have been the outer east wall of the original tower.

Be this as it may, Fairnilee is now a three-storeyed tower with crowstepped gables, with a conical-roofed angle-turret at the south-west corner, its corbelling decorated with an unusual upper course of archlike character. There are quatre-foil shot-holes beneath its windows. The present door, to the south, is a window enlargement, and opens into an unvaulted basement chamber with a large moulded fireplace. There has been a turnpike stair in the north-east angle, but only its well remains. At the south-east a moulded doorway admits to a vaulted passage or narrow cellar. This projects beyond the aforementioned dividing wall, which tends to invalidate the idea that this western portion was free-standing. A fragment of vaulting east of the stair-well also poses a structural problem.

The first floor, now reached by an outside forestair, has been greatly altered, with floor and ceiling levels changed, this requiring the turret, actually on the next floor level, to be reached from here by steps. The building internally, therefore, is of little interest, but the exterior is authentic, attractive and well maintained. A heraldic panel from above the former central doorway is now built into the north front bearing the arms of Rutherford impaling Ker, with an illegible motto.

A charter by Andrew Ker of Linton was granted at 'Phairnilee' in 1599, and in 1542 Mark Ker had rights in one of the Ettrick Forest steads called Fairniley. In 1722 the property is described as 'a very fine house with fine orchards avenues parks and planting, very pleasant'. It was here that Alison Rutherford, Mrs Patrick Cockburn, wrote her famous rendering of the ancient ballad, 'The Flowers of the Forest'.

## FAWSIDE CASTLE, EAST LOTHIAN

Possibly Fawside, sitting squarely on the summit of the long green ridge behind Wallyford, above the busy A1 highway west of Tranent, is one of the best-known landmarks in the Lothians; yet comparatively few know even its name, and fewer still have visited it. Like so many castles, it was recently under threat of demolition, but thanks to the initiative of certain private individuals it has been saved and a committee set up to preserve it—a heartening effort which might serve as a model for many another.

The castle, though long ruinous, survives in its main features, and has had an interesting development. Formerly enclosed within a courtyard, it originally consisted of a tall and fairly plain tower of the 15th century, containing four main storeys, of which the topmost was vaulted. Then, after the Battle of Pinkie, in which it suffered greatly, it was enlarged by the addition of a 16th-century extension to the south, of similar size and height, but L-shaped, doubling the accommodation. This wing has a stair-turret in the re-entrant angle and typical corner turrets corbelled out at the two southern angles. The 15th-century keep would be surmounted by the usual parapet and wall-walk, but this has disappeared. The walling is massive and there are few external features here. The entrance was by a rounded doorway in the north front, and a turnpike stairway rose in the north-east angle. The Hall on the first floor contained a fine lintelled fireplace in the south wall; and there have been garderobes and mural chambers. The vaulted roofing survives.

The 16th-century wing is more ornate and less substantial, and provides an excellent example of the French influence in Scottish castellated architecture introduced so dramatically by the Regent Mary of Guise and her daughter Mary Queen of Scots, in the provision of decorative corbelling, turrets, dormer pediments, window mouldings, relieving arches, and so on. The windows are much larger and more numerous, and some still contain their iron grilles. The entrance here was in the re-entrant angle, as usual. The foot of the stair-turret nearby is of unusual construction. The south-west angle of the extension is bevelled off, for improved defence. Internally this wing is wholly ruinous, all floors have fallen in, as has the basement vaulting.

Fawside, being so prominent on the main invasion route from the south to the capital, not unnaturally had a stirring history. A family of de Fauside, or de Falsyde, were settled here as early as 1150, but they were vassals of the great barony of Tranent nearby. Bruce granted this barony to his nephew Alexander de Seton, after the Wars of Independence, but the Fawsides remained in their tower, paying a reddendo of 1 lb of pepper or 2s. sterling —if asked for! At least one of them was armour-bearer to his Seton lord. The day before the Battle of Pinkie, in 1547, we read from an English source that the occupants of this castle shot at the invaders 'with hand-guns and hakbutts till the battle lost, when they pluct in their peces lyke a dog his taile, and couched themselfes within, all muet; but by and by the hous was set on fyre and they, for their good will, brent and smoothered within'. Hence the need for the 16th-century rebuilding. The Fawsides retained possession until 1631, when their castle was sold to an Edinburgh merchant burgess named Hamilton.

# GALDENOCH CASTLE, WIGTOWNSHIRE

This is a simple and unpretentious L-planned tower of the mid-16th century, very representative of its kind, long a ruin but with the main features surviving. It is now surrounded by a farm-steading, about one mile west of Lochnaw and seven miles north-west of Stranraer. It is notable for the small stones with which it is constructed, even the crowsteps of the gables being of composite construction, with a slate on top. The corbelling of the turret, and other worked stone, is of pinkish hue. The building is of three main storeys with an attic above, but the stair-wing to the north-east rises a storey higher, to finish in the usual small watch-chamber, formerly reached by a tiny turret stair. A circular angle-turret, with shot-holes, surmounts the south-west gable. The windows are small, and one lighting the stair-wing at first-floor level has an ogival head. There is a small shot-hole nearby.

The door is in the usual position within the re-entrant angle at the foot of the stair-wing, and is surmounted by a relieving arch. There is a small renewed panel in the main east walling nearby, with the initials G.A. and the date 1547. The entrance, defended by a draw-bar and socket, gives access to the foot of the turnpike stair, and also to the vaulted basement chamber. This is lighted by two slit windows only, but there is a built-up gunloop. There are two aumbries and a small fireplace. The Hall on the first floor, measuring 21 by 14 feet, is better lit, and there is a large fireplace, 9 feet wide, with two garderobes in the north wall and another recess in the south-west angle. A small turnpike stair, only 4 feet

in diameter, rises from the ingoing of a window near the south-east angle, giving access to the upper floors. This stairway is corbelled out internally, instead of the normal external projection, most unusual. There has been the normal sleeping accommodation higher.

Galdenoch, as might be expected, so close to the main Agnew stronghold of Lochnaw, belonged to that family, whose chiefs were Hereditary Sheriffs of Wigtownshire. It was built between 1547-50 by Gilbert Agnew, second son of Andrew of Lochnaw, who fell at the Battle of Pinkie. His grandson Patrick Agnew succeeded his father in 1635 and was fined £1,000 for refusing to embrace episcopacy. This branch of the family seems to have been brought to ruin about the end of the 17th century by the heavy fines inflicted for support of the Covenant, and by heavy losses sustained in the attempt to establish salt-pans on the nearby coast.

## GARLETON CASTLE, EAST LOTHIAN

The once-extensive 16th-century castle of Garleton, or Garmylton, is picturesquely situated under the north flank of the steep East Garleton Hill two miles west of Athelstaneford. The original structure has comprised three separate buildings around a courtyard, the main L-shaped block, of which little now remains, occupying the east front, with two detached wings projecting westwards to north and south. That to the north-west has been reduced to farm-cottages, though three of its gunloops still decorate the walling. The south-west house, however, as in sketch, is still entire although slightly altered.

It is oblong on plan, two storeys and a garret in height, with crowstepped gables and with a circular stair-tower projecting to the south, though this has been reduced in height and now has an oversailing roof. The original windows are small, and one at ground level to the south is still provided with its iron grille. A number have been built up. A feature is the number of wide splayed gunloops.

The basement contains two vaulted chambers which have formerly intercommunicated. That to the east is entered from the original door near the north-east angle, and contains a fireplace which has been hooded, a corbel for the support of which remains. The western chamber has been a kitchen with a wide arched fireplace built up in the partition wall. A wide modern doorway has been opened into this from the west. The stair has been removed

and there is now only an outside forestair. Internally the upper part of the house has been entirely modernised.

Portions of the former curtain-wall of the castle remain. Fragments of a large circular tower, formerly attached to the wing of the main house, still rise above the east curtain.

Garleton was early a property of the Lindsay family, and Sir David Lindsay of the Mount, the famous 16th-century playwright, Lord Lyon and tutor of James the Fifth, is thought to have been born here. Later it passed to the family of Towers of Inverleith, from whom it was acquired by the 3rd Earl of Winton, who bestowed it on his fourth son, in the early 17th century, who thus founded the family of Seton of Garleton. It is now part of the farm-steading.

## GREENAN CASTLE, AYRSHIRE

Most dramatically situated on a cliff-top promontary two miles south of Ayr, Greenan is a well-known landmark. It is a simple oblong tower of composite date, said to have been erected by John Kennedy of Baltersan in 1603—the initials J.K. and the date 1603 featured near the doorway. But there was a previous fortalice on the site, and much of the present work appears to pre-date the early 17th century. The walls measure 35 by 28 feet and rise four storeys, to end in now roofless angle-turrets at three corners, the fourth having been occupied by the caphouse and stair-head, at the north-west angle, now much broken-down. There is no parapet. There has been a courtyard to the east, part of the curtain-

walling for which remains, on the south side, and a deep ditch has
protected the approach from landward. There has been a plinth
or basement course around the seaward sides of the tower. The
building is now unfortunately in a bad state of repair.

The entrance, at basement level, is by a doorway at the edge of
the cliff facing north, and is now built up. It must always have
been precarious of access. The basement is vaulted. There has been
a first-floor entrance, no doubt reached by a removable timber
stair from the courtyard, to the east, and it is interesting to note
that the heraldic panel-space which is normally above the basement doorway, is here inserted alongside the first-floor doorway
—since it would be somewhat wasted in the normal position to
the north, where no caller could stand back far enough to look
up at it. The Hall, on the first floor, measures 25 by 20 feet, and
has a large fireplace and windows on all sides. The second floor
was similar, and the top storey was an attic one, with dormers, and
shot-holes in the turrets.

In the 15th century, Greenan was in the hands of the Davidson
family, but in 1588 John Davidson of Greenan sold certain lands
to John Kennedy of Baltersan. Possibly his wife, Margaret Kennedy, was related to Baltersan, for we find that laird in possession
of Greenan in 1596. It was in this castle that Sir Thomas Kennedy,

of nearby Culzean, younger son of Gilbert, 3rd Earl of Cassillis, spent the night of 11th May 1602, before his celebrated murder by Mure of Auchendrane.

## HERMITAGE CASTLE, ROXBURGHSHIRE

The famous castle of Hermitage stands remotely in a branch valley of Liddesdale, four miles north of Newcastleton. Although long a roofless ruin, it is intact to the wallhead, well cared-for by the Ministry of Works, and deservedly a magnet for visitors to the Borderland, for it constitutes one of the finest examples of Scottish mediaeval castellated architecture. Although it ranked as a military strength, it was always in private hands and therefore may be termed a fortified house.

Although it looks fairly homogeneous, Hermitage dates from four main periods. It consists of a 14th-century central main block, with large towers projecting at the four angles, the wing to the south-west being much larger than the others as well as later. The excellent coursed ashlar walls rise to four main storeys, and crowstepped gables of the 16th century still surmount the east elevation. The east and west sides of the main block are notable for the tall archways which link their towers. There has been a timber gallery, or *bretache*, projecting round the building at third-floor level, the socket holes for which remain. The wallhead and parapet were reconstructed in the 19th century.

The nucleus was a small courtyard castle of the late 13th century, traces of which remain. After 1383 this was built up into a much larger oblong, the present main block, lying east and west, with a small wing projecting at the south-west angle. Shortly afterwards, larger square towers were added at each of the other angles; and about 1400 the south-west tower was extended into a long, tall wing. There have been only slight alterations since. The wide splayed gunloops, are however, of the 16th century. There are a few machicolated projections. The windows are small and irregularly placed, save at third-floor level. There has been a garret storey, now gone.

The entrance doorway is in the centre of the south front, with a postern in the south-east tower. This main door is a later addition, the original having been at first-floor level in the early south-west tower, with portcullis protection. Above the present main door, at parapet level, is a gabled machicolation for its defence. The entrance leads into a little central court, part of the

original castle. Doorways open to large unvaulted chambers at either side, and, at the north end, to a mural turnpike stair. Access has at a later date been slapped through from the corner of the east apartment into the well-chamber in the foot of the south-east tower. The basements of the other towers are not reachable from this level.

The stair rises only to the first floor, and as there is now no other stair, how the upper floors were reached remains uncertain. There were two apartments in the main block at this level, the larger to the west, the public hall, that to the east, the private hall. From the latter there is access to the two towers, that to the north-east containing the pit or prison, that to the south-east having a service-stair down to the well-chamber. From the larger hall the north-west tower and south-west wing are reached, the latter containing a large ill-lit apartment with a straight stair down to the kitchen below, the only access. Here is a wide fireplace, and oven, with a drain nearby for slops.

The second floor of the main block was originally one great chamber, but it has been partitioned. Apartments in the towers at this level are similar to below, all having garderobes off, that in the south-east tower partly in a corbelled-out projection. The third floor is similar, though notable for its many and regular windows.

The original Hermitage was apparently built by Sir Nicholas de Soulis, Lord of Liddesdale, before the Wars of Independence. A descendant, Sir John, was one of the Guardians of Scotland during that desperate period. Sir William de Soulis was forfeited for high treason in 1320, and Robert the Bruce gave Hermitage to his own illegitimate son Robert. During the puppet-king Edward Baliol's reign the castle was handed over to the English, but in 1342 Sir William Douglas, the celebrated Knight of Liddesdale and Flower of Chivalry, took it and somewhat blotted his escutcheon by starving to death therein Sir Alexander Ramsay. William, 1st Earl of Douglas gained Hermitage, and it remained with the Black Douglas line until the collapse of that great house, when it passed to the Red Douglases of Angus. James the Fourth gave it to Patrick Hepburn, Earl of Bothwell, whose descendants held it until it was acquired by the burgeoning house of Scott of Buccleuch, with whom it still remains. During all these vicissitudes it was frequently the scene of stirring action, often treasonable, its proximity to the Borderline making it a vital key to power.

## INNERPEFFRAY CASTLE, PERTHSHIRE

In a picturesque but not very strong position on sloping ground above a bend of the River Earn four miles south-east of Crieff, and near the more famous Innerpeffray Library, this is a commodious but plain fortified mansion of the early 17th century, now a roofless ruin but more or less complete to the wallhead. It is built on the L-plan, with a square stair-tower in the re-entrant angle, the main block being three storeys in height and the wing a storey higher. The walls are of coursed rubble with dressed quoins, the basement openings being mere slits, while the first-floor windows are notably large. Gunloops command the entrance, at ground- and above first-floor levels. There are no turrets. The chimney-stacks are notable, that at the wing gable, containing the kitchen flue, being large and massive, leaving room for only six crowsteps at the sides; while that serving the Hall fireplace rises from the wallhead in tall isolation on the west front. A courtyard has extended to north and west, part of the door-jamb for which still survives.

The doorway is in the foot of the stair-tower and admits to an entrance lobby, wherein is a stone bench for a porter, below the stair, and a shot-hole to command the entrance. The ingoing of this has been utilised to act as a sort of service-hatch from kitchen to stair-foot. The basement is vaulted, with the kitchen in the wing provided with a wide arched fireplace which has an oven at one end and a stone seat and aumbry at the other. There is also a stone drain—a provision also to be found in the adjoining larder.

The vaulted chamber at the north end of the main block has been the laird's wine-cellar, with a private stair in the walling to the Hall above.

The main turnpike stair is wide and admits to all floors. The Hall is as usual on the first floor, and has been a fine room measuring 32 by 20 feet, and lit by the large windows on three sides. The masonry above the great fireplace in the west wall has been strengthened with a relieving arch, visible from outside. A private room adjoins the Hall, provided with garderobe and aumbry, and there was a bedroom in the wing at this level. Above, the arrangement was the same, with a withdrawing-room instead of the Hall, a comparatively late development.

Innerpeffray, like so much of Strathearn, was a Drummond lairdship. Much of the land hereabouts was Church property, belonging to the Abbey of Inchaffray, and at the Reformation the Drummonds saw to it that one of their number was secular Commendator. The lands were erected into a temporal lordship for the said James Drummond, younger and infant son of the 2nd. Lord Drummond, and in 1609 he was created Lord Madderty. He built Innerpeffray the following year. The renowned Library nearby was endowed by a bequest of David, 3rd Lord Madderty in 1691, and contains many rare and interesting books, including the pocket-Bible of the great Marquis of Montrose. Close to the Library is Innerpeffray Chapel which, since 1508, has been the burial-ground of the Drummonds.

# JOHNSTONE CASTLE, RENFREWSHIRE

Now rising gauntly amongst the streets of a modern housing scheme built in the former policies of the estate, to the south of the burgh of Johnstone, this castle has had a chequered career. Originally the fortalice was named Easter Cochran and owned by the family of that Ilk, one of whom was ennobled as Lord Cochrane of Dundonald, in 1647, and Earl of Dundonald in 1669. It was acquired however by the Houstons of Johnstone, across the River Black Cart, in 1733, who disposed of their previous property but brought the name of Johnstone across the river to bestow on this castle. The Houstons greatly added to and altered the former mainly 16th-century fortalice in the years that followed, 'gothicising' it in unsightly fashion. Now, the estate taken over by the burgh, most of the extended mansion has been pulled down and only the original left, though unfortunately itself much scarred by 19th-century 'improvements'. The building is now used as a store in connection with the burgh services.

The castle as it now stands is L-shaped, and consists of a comparatively little-altered main block of three storeys and a garret, lying east and west, with a wing, now built in the form of a massive Gothic tower, projecting northwards and rising a storey higher. The more authentic main block has a number of features. A two-storeyed angle-turret crowns the east gable to the north, and no doubt contained a small turret-stair to give access to the rather unusual watch-chamber which projects on corbelling in the re-entrant angle. The roof-line of both turret and watch-chamber has been altered in unsightly manner. A squared shot-hole opens from the lower part of the turret. Notable is the very massive chimney-stack of this east gable, housing the kitchen flue. An empty heraldic panel-space, surrounded by a rope-moulding, is situated in an unusual and lofty position below watch-chamber and turret.

The doorway is in the re-entrant at the foot of the north wing or tower, and above, at second-floor level, are two large corbels for a machicolated projection from which a drastic welcome could be poured down upon unwelcome visitors. The doorway is guarded also by an arrow-slit to the left. Apart from two tiny windows at basement level, and others built up, the wing has been so altered as not to be worth describing.

The entrance has a vaulted porter's lodge, and opens on to a vaulted passage, from the left end of which the main block basement chambers are reached. The kitchen occupies the east end, and

has a great wide-arched fireplace in the gable. The vault to the west was the wine-cellar, with the usual private stairway in the thickness of the south-west walling, to the floor above. Here, as ever, was the Hall, now greatly altered but still retaining a garde-robe and a very deep window embrasure—which gives the impression of a nucleus older than the 16th century. The vaulted basement corridor into the north wing is now walled off, and this area otherwise altered; but no doubt originally it would give access to the main stairway. The upper floors were inaccessible.

## CASTLE KENNEDY, WIGTOWNSHIRE

This tall and impressive castle, set amongst the well-known gardens of the Earl of Stair's property of Lochinch, about four miles east of Stranraer, is less ancient than it is apt to appear. Strongly-sited on a ridge of ground between two lochs, it dates only from the early 17th century. Considering its size, and the importance of its builder, it is remarkably plain as to external appearance, although the plan is elaborate and unusual. It consists of a main block, four storeys and an attic in height, with two square wings projecting at the north-east and south-east corners, slightly higher; and within the re-entrant angles created by these, to the west, two further square towers rise to a still greater height, seven storeys, that to the south containing the main turnpike stairway. At a slightly later date, lower three-storey wings were

added to north and west. The building has long been a roofless ruin, and unfortunately heavy ivy growth obscures much of the exterior. The windows are fairly large and regularly placed, and one in the south wing has its iron yett or grille still in place. There are a number of circular shot-holes. The only decorative feature is a fine dormer window and pediment on the north wall-head of the north wing.

The main entrance was in the east front, recessed between the two wings, leading into a vaulted basement passage running westwards through the entire building. On the north side, a door opens into the large vaulted kitchen, measuring 30 by 14 feet, with a water inlet and two aumbries, but, oddly, no fireplace. The basement rooms in the square wings or towers are also vaulted. The wide stair in the south tower is entered from the vaulted passage. The upper storeys are now inaccessible but would be on a handsome scale undoubtedly, and commodious, with the usual arrangement of Hall and public rooms on the first floor and sleeping accommodation higher.

The lands, formerly belonging to the Church, probably the Abbey of Soulseat, came into the Kennedy's acquisitive hands in 1482, and this castle was commenced, but not finished, in 1607 by John, 5th Earl of Cassillis, replacing an older keep. It did not long remain with the family which named it however, for they suffered greatly, financially and otherwise, for their support of the Covenant, and Castle Kennedy passed, about 1677, to Sir John Dalrymple, Lord President of the Court of Session, later Viscount Stair, head of that up-and-coming house. It was accidently gutted by fire in 1716 and never restored. The handsome grounds surrounding it were laid out in the Dutch style by Field-Marshal the Earl of Stair, who died in 1747.

## KIRKLAND-DUNLOP, AYRSHIRE

This most attractive small 16th-century house, in Dunlop village, although without any recognisable ecclesiastical features, was the original pre-Reformation Vicarage of Dunlop, an important benefice of Kilwinning Abbey, and is notable as being the residence of the famous Master John Major, scholar and historian, teacher of Knox and other Reformers, who was Vicar here from 1518 until 1550—although also Professor of Theology at Glasgow and St. Andrews and Treasurer of the Chapel-Royal; whatever his reforming tendencies, he seems to have taken full advantage of the deplorable system of plurality of offices!

The building, which has been much altered and restored, is typical, L-shaped, steep-roofed with crowstepped gables, and a circular stair-tower with conical roof within the re-entrant angle. There are now only two storeys, but there may have once been an additional garret within the roof. The walls, from 3 to 4 feet thick, are of good coursed rubble and rise from massive boulder foundations. There is a good eaves-course. The house has been extended to the east, most of the windows have been enlarged and some built-up, but one small light on the north side retains its original roll-moulding. The entrance, formerly in the foot of the stair-tower, has been reduced to a window, and a new door

opened close by in the main block. An interesting stone drainage-spout projects above, surmounting a corbel carved as a mask An illustration in a book of 1885 shows the house with roof over-sailing tower and dormers.

Internally there has been very considerable alteration, ancient and modern. There is no vaulting. A small aumbry or cavity remains beside the former doorway at the foot of the turnpike stair; and there is another aumbry in the walling upstairs. The old kitchen was in the wing to the west of the door, at ground level. The minister's study above has had a large fireplace, and it is said that its heavy lintel has been defaced, probably to remove Popish symbols at the Reformation. There is much panelling of later date.

Formerly the Vicarage must have been practically a small laird-ship, with about 40 acres of land attached. In 1566, at the Reformation, these lands, save for an acre retained for the last Catholic Vicar, Master John Houston, were granted to Cunningham of Aiket. The Vicarage became the Manse, and so remained until 1781, when a new one was built, and the old building became a farmhouse. It was later restored as a small mansion, and is now in excellent repair and lovingly cherished.

## KNOCKDOLIAN CASTLE, AYRSHIRE

Standing high above the River Stinchar, close to the modern mansion of the same name, about a mile west of Colmonell, this sturdy and attractive tower of the 16th century, though no longer habitable, is in a fair state of repair, and is unusual in certain respects. Oblong on plan, measuring 35 by 25 feet, it rises four storeys to a parapet and walk, with a garret storey above. The parapet however crowns only the east and west wallheads, and has this peculiarity that it projects on continuous corbelling on the west front, while the more elementary individual corbels carry it on the east or river side. There are open rounds at the ends, and the usual cannon-like spouts for drainage. The turnpike stair, which rises in the north-west angle, ends at parapet-level in a rounded caphouse, now roofless. The windows are fairly small, the basement being lit by keyhole-type slits, and there is a large shot-hole at first-floor level in the east wall. At this level a small stair-window to the west is surmounted by a panel with shield, much weather-worn but apparently dated 16??. There has been a courtyard to north and west.

The door, in the west front, admits to a basement of two

vaulted cellars, and to the wheel stair. The Hall, on the first floor, has a large fireplace in the centre of the west wall, for which a tall chimney-stack rises at parapet-level.

Knockdolian was a property of the Grahame family. Sir John Grahame of Knockdolian married Helen, eldest daughter of Thomas Kennedy of Bargany in the 16th century. The property later passed to the family of McCubbin, possibly through marriage, for Fergus McCubbin and his wife, another Margaret Kennedy, made extensive repairs to the castle in the mid-17th century. No doubt the aforementioned heraldic panel refers to this, and it may account for the different treatment of the wallhead at east and west sides. This sort of parapet feature is late, for the mid-17th century, but situated in the midst of the turbulent Kennedy country, with feud and outrage prevalent for considerably after this, any prudent laird was well advised to look to his defences.

## CASTLE LEVAN, RENFREWSHIRE

Situated on a high bank above the Clyde coast, about three miles south-west of Gourock, and in the grounds of a more modern mansion, this is an interesting building, long ruinous but with the main features surviving. It is somewhat unusual as to plan, being a variation of the L but with the two wings joining only at one corner each. Indeed it seems probable that the castle dates from two periods, and that the original, that to the north, was a simple 15th-century tower, and that a somewhat larger keep was

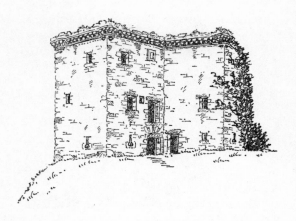

added to the south-east in the early 16th century, of the same height and general style of architecture, and in such fashion as to provide two deep re-entrants. As it now stands, Levan is a well-constructed double tower of three storeys and a garret, with very thick walls, having a parapet and walk carried on handsome chequered corbelling, with open rounds at the angles, the windows being notably small. There are a number of keyhole-type arrow-slits. The site is a very strong one on the edge of a deep and steep ravine.

There are actually three entrances to the north, all in the re-entrant angle, that in the foot of the north tower being modern. Of the other two, in the south tower, that at ground level and exceedingly low-set, was probably only an access to the basement cellars, with the one above, at first-floor level the main entrance, and reached by a removable timber stairway. This upper doorway appears to have been enlarged. High above, just below the parapet, is an empty panel-space. The extreme north-west corner of the north tower is shattered and partially collapsed.

The basement is vaulted in both sections, and contains kitchen, wine-cellar and storage, with two narrow straight stairs in the thickness of the walling leading to the Hall, which occupies the first floor of the southern tower. There has been a turnpike stair contrived in the corner where the two wings join. The upper floors have now fallen in.

Castle Levan belonged originally to a family called Morton, before passing to the Sempills—who were of course prominent in Renfrewshire from the 14th century. Still later it was acquired by the Shaw-Stewarts of nearby Inverkip, with which castle it has not a few similarities. Adam Morton of Lavane, cadet of the Mortons of East Walkingshaw, sold the property to William, 2nd Lord Sempill previous to 1539. However, when in that year Sempill got the lands of Lavane incorporated in the free barony of Sempill, for some reason this displeased James, the son of Adam Morton, who raised an action against Sempill to interdict him from 'uplifting the mails, fermes, proffittis and dewties of the landis of Lavenbrayis'. Sempill won in the protracted litigation. In 1649 it was acquired by the Stewarts.

## MAYSHIEL, EAST LOTHIAN

Remotely set, high amongst the Lammermoors, in Whittinghame parish, about five miles south of Garvald, this is a small and simple bonnet-laird's house of the 17th century, now a farm-place accommodating a shepherd's family. It has a distinct resemblance to the similar house of Johnscleuch, a few miles to the north. Rising from massive boulder foundations, this is an L-shaped house, of main block and stair-tower, containing two storeys and a garret, the roof of which has been lowered and made less steep. The walls are roughcast and very thick, the corners being rounded. Most of the windows have been enlarged, but the small stair light is original, as is the upper floor window in the east gable, which has a simple roll moulding. The chimney-stack at the west gable is fairly massive. The lowering of the stair-tower roof is somewhat unsightly.

The entrance is by a high arched doorway in the re-entrant angle, guarded by a large gunloop in the stair-tower, with an unusual rectangular splay. The doorway and the window above are set in a slight outwards bulge, which is unusual. The interior has been wholly altered and adapted to present requirements and no features of interest remain other than the fairly wide turnpike stair in the tower, and the ingoing for the gunloop. That the stair has risen higher is evidenced by the cut-off tread above the first floor landing. The basement is not vaulted. There has been a courtyard to the south, part of the buttressed walling for which remains to the east.

Mayshiel is a very old name. There is an early reference to the property in the records of the island Priory of The May, which records that the lands 'in the Lambermor' were granted to the Priory by John Fitz-Michael, reputed ancestor of the Wemyss family. No date is given for this grant, but there is another grant

mentioned of the neighbouring property of Penshiel, from the
Cospatrick Earl of Dunbar and March, in 1200. It may be that
the name of Mayshiel is derived from this island link. The pro-
perty remained church lands down till the Reformation. In 1583
William Stewart, Captain of the King's Guard, second son of
Thomas Stewart of Galston (Garlieston?) obtained a gift of the
lands and Priory of Pittenweem, which had superseded the May
Island establishment, and was styled Commendator, Mayshiel in
Lothian being listed amongst the properties. In 1606 the title of
Commendator Prior was dropped and the lands wholly secu-
larised, being erected into a temporal barony in favour of his son,
Frederick Stewart, who was styled Lord Pittenweem, the lands
of Mayshiel, with the tiend-sheaves thereof being specifically in
the relevant Act of Parliament. Lord Pittenweem feud Mayshiel
to William Cockburn of that Ilk, thereafter. There are references
to changes of ownership, in the Register of the Great Seal, in
1612 and 1615, in the name of Dishington and of Thomas,
Viscount Fentoun (Sir Thomas Erskine, of Gowrie Conspiracy
fame); but Cockburn of that Ilk seems to have obtained ownership
eventually, as well as possession, for in 1656 the Lord Protector
Cromwell confirms a charter to Richard Cairns of Pilmuir, by
William Cockburn of that Ilk, of 'the lands of Mayshill, in the
parish of Whittinghame'.

# MERVINSLAW TOWER, ROXBURGHSHIRE

Standing high on the steep bare hillside above the deep dean of the Peel Burn, and overlooking the larger valley of the Jed Water about six miles south of Jedburgh, this strongly situated little fortalice is a roofless ruin, but complete to the wallhead and better preserved than most neighbouring peel-towers. Though simple of construction, it has one or two features of interest. Oblong on plan and based on a steeply-sloping site, it is of three storeys, with the gables to north and south approximately. The rubble masonry is rough but substantial, and enhanced by more dressed freestone at the openings than might be expected. The basement course is of the usual large boulders.

There are two doors, both well revetted and backset, provided with deep double bar-holes. The few windows are tiny, but that to the north of the main doorway at first-floor level has a simple roll moulding. This doorway would be reached by the usual removable timber stair. The other door gave access only to the basement chamber, and is in the south gable; and above is a square protective shot-hole and tiny window. Higher in the south gable, at attic level, is another small window. There are simple relieving arches over both doorways. This south gable is slightly intaken at attic level.

The interior is now open to the sky. The basement has not been vaulted, and the joist-holes and corbels for the support of timber floors remain. There are a number of small aumbries. There is no internal stairway, so access to the attic floor must have been by

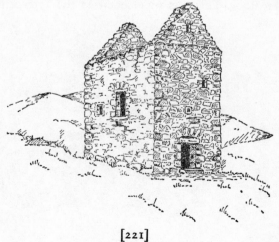

ladder from the first floor. Oddly enough there is no fireplace nor flue in the building, but there are the foundations of subsidiary courtyard buildings to the south, and as in some other peel-towers, these must have been used for general living, with the tower as an insurance against attack. The building appears to date from the 16th century, and measures 25 by 21 feet.

This was an Oliver house, like others nearby—Edgerston, Slacks, and so on. In 1572 we read that Will Oliver of Lustruther stood caution for Oliver in Mervinslaw and others of the name. No doubt, being only a very few miles from the English border, at Carter Bar, this little tower saw a great deal of action and bloodshed.

## MONTQUHANIE CASTLE, FIFE

Set in the quiet north-east Fife parish of Kilmany, five miles north of Cupar, Montquhanie is a picturesque composition of 15th-century keep and late 16th-century and later additions, near the modern mansion. The keep is ruinous but the courtyard wing to the west is still entire, indeed recently restored, and occupied, as an attractive small dower-house.

The keep, which has been somewhat altered, is oblong and rises four storeys to a parapet and walk with open rounds at three angles. The original windows are notably small. There is no communication between the basement and the upper floors; so that the original door would be reached by a removable timber stair to the first floor. This was superseded, in the 17th century, by a

handsome stone forestair from the courtyard, to the north. There is now no internal stairway, but there is a large gap in the north walling where it probably arose in a projecting tower. As neither of the two basement vaults has a fireplace, the kitchen premises must always have been in secondary courtyard buildings. The Hall, on the first floor, has a fireplace in each gable, and there are two lighted closets. The upper floors are inaccessible.

The west curtain-wall of the courtyard is incorporated in the occupied extension, built on slanting, rocky ground which dictates irregular floor-levels. It consists of a small circular flanking-tower with a conical roof, and a long two storeyed-range with crowstepped gabling. The tower, its upper part formerly used as a dovecote, is furnished with splayed gunloops of late 16th-century type, and its upper window is provided with a drip-stone. The rest of the building appears to date from about a century later.

McGibbon & Ross state that there was a heraldic lintel erected upside-down in an outbuilding, showing the Balfour arms, the initials A.B. for Andrew Balfour, and dated 1597. This could well have been the period of the flanking tower and first extensions.

'Moulhany' was exchanged by the last Earl of Fife, in the early 14th century, for Pittencrieff, with his kinsman Michael Balfour. In 1458 George Balfour signed a charter at 'Munquhane'. His grandson, Sir Michael, a favourite of James the Fourth and dying with him at Flodden, left an infant son, Andrew (above referred to) who was laird for 79 years. He had eight sons, all distinguished during the reigns of James the Fifth, Mary Queen of Scots, and James the Sixth. The third and fourth sons were respectively involved in the murders of Darnley and Cardinal Beaton. The old laird was succeeded by his great-gransdon, Sir Andrew, and the estate sold about 1600. The new lairds were Lumsdens of the Innergellie line, and Major-General Robert Lumsden, a veteran of the Gustavus Adolphus wars, was captured at the Battle of Dunbar and 'very hardlie used'; appointed Governor of Dundee in 1651, and when he surrendered to the Cromwellians on honourable terms, was nevertheless slain by the English soldiery. His son sold Montquhanie to James Crawford, of the Ayrshire Auchinames family in 1676. A stone built-in to the fabric is dated 1682 with initials I.C. and M.L.

# PINWHERRY CASTLE, AYRSHIRE

Crowning a defensive mound in the attractive castle-dotted valley of the Stinchar, in the hamlet of the same name about five miles from Colmonell, this is a ruinous late 16th-century fortalice on the L-plan, now in a bad state of repair but with the main features surviving, some of them very interesting. It consists of a main block lying east and west, with a stair-wing extending northwards, to end in a gabled watch-chamber. A squared stair-turret of unusual design projects in the re-entrant above first-floor level, and a single circular angle-turret, now very fragmentary, crowns the south-west corner. A tall and substantial chimney-stack rises above the north wallhead, and there is an empty heraldic panel-space above the doorway, which is in the usual position at the foot of the stair-wing in the re-entrant. This door has been provided with a bar-hole and a lamp recess. There are three main storeys beneath the wallhead and the wing rises a storey higher. The gables are crowstepped.

The interior is now largely fallen-in and inaccessible. The basement has been vaulted, and in the south-west corner there is a small circular stair to the Hall above, in addition to the main turnpike in the wing. The Hall contained a large fireplace in the north wall, the flue for which is accommodated in the large stack already mentioned. The sleeping quarters higher were reached by the turret stair. There has been a courtyard to the north.

Pinwherry has been variously spelt in its long story. The laird,

in 1596, presumably the builder, was John Kennedy of 'Banqu-harrie'. The last of this branch of the turbulent Carrick Kennedies was Thomas, of Pinwherry who died in 1644. In 1648 we read that the property belonged to John, Earl of Carrick. Later it came into the hands of the Pollock family.

## PLUNTON CASTLE, KIRKCUDBRIGHTSHIRE

Remotely situated amongst green knowes on the farm of Lennox Plunton about three miles south-east of Gatehouse-of-Fleet and two miles north-west of Borgue, this is a fairly typical L-planned tower-house of the second half of the 16th century, long ruinous and neglected but still retaining its main features. The masonry is rough but strong, but the simplicity of the whole is enriched by the comparatively elaborate corbelling of the three angle tur-rets, two of which survive almost intact. There are three main storeys beneath the wallhead, with an attic above, and a turnpike stair rose in the small wing which projects at the south-west corner. There are relieving arches over certain of the windows. Unfortunately most of the dressed stone has been torn out of late years. There are rudimentary gunloops and a few shot-holes.

The entrance is, as usual, in the re-entrant angle at the foot of the stair, and gives access also to the southern of the two vaulted basement chambers. The cellar to the north has been entered from a separate door from the courtyard to the west, an unusual ar-rangement since it detracts from security. The chambers are lit

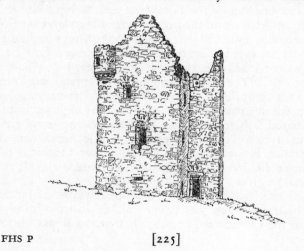

only by slits. The Hall on the first floor measures 23 by 15 feet, and has windows on all sides and a wide fireplace in the west wall. The two upper floors have been subdivided into four bedrooms, each with a fireplace. The turrets were reached from the attic floor, for the defensive cover of all walling.

Unfortunately the building is in a poor state, and the stairway has gone.

Plunton was a seat of a branch of the well-known Galloway family of McGhie, in the early 16th century, but passed to a family called Lennox towards the middle of that century. It would seem, therefore, that the present building was of Lennox erection; indeed in 1684 Symson describes it as 'a good strong house, called the Castle of Plunton-Lennox'. Sir Walter Scott used it as the scene of his *Doom of Devorgoil*.

## RAVENSCRAIG CASTLE, FIFE

Dramatically set on a cliff-top above the shore midway between Kirkcaldy and Dysart, this highly interesting castle is now overlooked by the high flats of the former town's expansion. It is unusual in many respects, and is said to have been the first castle in Scotland specifically designed to withstand artillery-fire, belonging to the 15th century with later additions. Partly because of the nature of the site, it does not conform to any normal plan. Two massive horseshoe-shaped towers lying to east and west are linked by a lower range, in which is the entrance, guarded by double doors, one slotted for a draw bar, and facing a bridge over a deep gully which cuts off the promontory site to landwards. The west tower seems much higher, being four storeys and an attic, while that to the east is a storey less; but because of the uneven level of the site to that side, two of its storeys are below basement level of the other. There has been considerable later work, in the 16th and 17th centuries, to seawards, terraced at varying levels, but this is wholly ruinous. The masonry throughout is of excellent squared ashlar, and the landward-facing semi-circular flanks of the two towers are of enormous thickness. A most interesting feature is the manner in which the west tower is tabled off with stone slabbing at what should be parapet level; this is probably not original.

The castle was built for Mary of Gueldres, widow of James the Second, about 1460, but was never finished in its original conception, for the Queen died in 1463. It thereupon was bestowed

on William St. Clair, Earl of Orkney, in partial compensation, when those islands were taken into the Scottish crown by James the Third, by the famous transaction with Norway, and the earldom changed to that of Caithness. This would account for the obvious alterations in style.

The entrance is by a narrow arched pend leading to an inner courtyard, in the lower linking building, which is in fact only one storey high, though landward its walling has been raised by a high parapet of immensely thick masonry, pierced by gunloops. On either side are vaulted cellars, and above is a platform roof, for cannon. The eastern and lower tower has a well cut in the rock floor of its vaulted basement, and the stairway is straight, in the thickness of the west wall. Its attic floor and parapet are of the 17th century.

The tall and massive western tower has been entered from a fore-stair at first-floor level, to the south, and a turnpike stairway rises nearby at its south-east angle. There is a comparatively small chamber on each floor, because of the wall thickness, and there are many mural cupboards and garderobes. Presumably this first floor would be the Hall, somewhat inadequate as it would be for an important castle—though almost certainly it was originally planned for the Hall to be above the basements of the connecting building, where there would have been ample room. The massive chimney-stack of the Hall fireplace flue is a prominent feature of the roofline.

It is good that this interesting building, long ruinous and neglected, is now being rehabilitated.

Ravenscraig remained long the seat of the Lords Sinclair, a senior offshoot of the Caithness earldom.

## SMEATON CASTLE, MIDLOTHIAN

Remarkably little known considering the scale of this once large courtyard-style castle, Smeaton, now going under the name of Dalkeith Home Farm, stands within the very north-east corner of the great policies of Dalkeith Palace, where the Smeaton Burn descends to join the Esk, about a mile south of Inveresk. It appears to have been an impressive establishment of possibly the 15th centuy, with later alterations, enclosing an oblong courtyard, with circular flanking-towers at the angles, of which only those at the north-west and south-west remain, with a main range of lower level along the south curtain-wall, now modernised. No traces of the eastern towers or perimeter walling on that side are now evident. Indications of the moat remain.

The dominant feature is the tall south-west tower, circular but with a square stair-tower attached to the east. Unfortunately this challenging composition, although entire to the eaves-course, has been given an unsuitable modern roof. It is now four storeys high, but the floor levels have been altered. It would rise a storey higher. The walls are thick, of good coursed rubble. Some of the windows have been much enlarged. There are two wide splayed gunloops facing north and south, now part-filled as ventilators. The stair-tower windows are original and tiny, and there has been a doorway at first floor level to the south, no doubt reached by a removable gangway across the moat, and later by a stone forestair now removed. The handsome plinth or basement course is notable. There are relieving arches over many of the windows.

The slightly smaller north-west tower has been reduced in height and completely altered internally. The basement chamber, which was not vaulted, has contained a moulded fireplace. The section of curtain-wall connecting these towers is interesting and substantial, with a series of fairly large windows, old but not original. Presumably a lean-to building has been erected here, possibly a large hall. The range along the south front, always the main dwelling-house, is now so altered externally as to retain no original features but the basement course and two small windows. Internally it is otherwise, the ground floor having a range of

four large vaulted chambers, plus that in the round tower. Certain of the partitions are modern, and possibly there were originally only three. That to the west may have been the wine-cellar, for there is a mural cupboard here, part-filling a larger aperture which might have housed the usual private stair from the Hall above. The partition with the next chamber is very wide, and probably contained the flue for a wide fireplace, which would indicate that the next apartment was the kitchen. There are no special features in the other vaults. There has been another turnpike stairway on the north front, now removed, its space incorporated in a modern passage.

The main newel-stair, rising in the square tower, is fairly narrow, with close garderobes off on the second and third floors. The upper tower rooms, as in the main house, are wholly modernised.

The lack of knowledge about Smeaton is puzzling. An early reference indicates these lands as belonging to the great Abbey of Dunfermline in 1450. At the Reformation period, Mary Queen of Scots, in 1563 confirmed a charter of Smetoun, with other lands, to Master Robert Richardson, Prior of St. Mary's Isle, in Galloway, a prominent cleric, indeed Treasurer of Scotland and member of the Privy Council. In 1576 another charter confirms Smetoun to James Richardson, natural son of the Treasurer, and Elizabeth Douglas his wife; and mentions the house, lands, messuage-place and fortalice thereof. The surviving buildings however indicate an earlier date than this. It is interesting to note that in 1644 there is a Privy Council reference to the ancient family of Richardson of Smetoun. It is hardly likely that its acquisition in 1563 would confer this description; so it is probable that there had been Richardsons at Smeaton long before the Treasurer found himself in a financial position to acquire them. That he accumulated much personal wealth is indicated by the efforts of the Privy Council long after his death, to recover royal jewellery etc., from his heirs. It is worth noting that in 1547, after the Battle of Pinkie, the English commander methodically destroyed all the substantial buildings of this area, including 16 mills—and of course nearby Fawside Castle. It is hardly likely that Smeaton escaped. Possibly it was the derelict property of his ancestors that the Treasurer restored. His son James was one of the Ruthven Raiders, who kidnapped King James the Sixth, in the troubled years of his youth. The grandson, Sir James Richardson of Smetoun, was prominent in affairs also, made Sheriff of Edinburghshire in 1615 and a bailie of Musselburgh. He and his father were more than once before the Privy Council on the complaints of 'the poor tenants' of their lands for raising the rents; and in 1604 Mark Aitchison, in Prestonpans, had to find security not to harm the James Richardsons, father and son—while the following year the situation was reversed and the Richardsons had to find caution for 2,000 merks not to assault Aitchison!

## SORBIE CASTLE, WIGTOWNSHIRE

The site of this castle, on level ground about a mile east of Sorbie village and five miles south of Wigtown, does not at first glance seem a strong one; but it is built on an artificial defensive mound, allegedly on the remains of an early Pictish fort, and amidst marshy ground—for the name, Sourby meant a dwelling amid swamps. This mound is now so closely grown with trees as to make both it and the castle scarcely discernible from any distance. The fortalice itself, while possibly incorporating more ancient work, dates mainly from the late 16th and early 17th centuries, and though long ruinous, ivy-grown and neglected, is now being given some attention.

It is an L-shaped building, more lofty and commodious than many of its kind, rising to three storeys and an attic in the main block, with the wing a storey higher to end in a gabled watch-chamber. There is no parapet and walk. A tall stair-turret rises within the re-entrant angle above first-floor level, the bottom

corbel of which is quaintly carved as a human head. There have been angle-turrets at the corners, now reduced to their corbelling. Unfortunately much of the dressed stone of the windows has been torn out.

The entrance is in the usual position within the re-entrant and is surmounted by an empty panel-space. The door was defended by no fewer than three draw-bars, the deep sockets for which remain. The basement consists of four vaulted apartments. The kitchen occupied the north end of the main block, and had an enormous arched fireplace in the gable, 17 feet wide by 5 deep, with a small window at one end and an aumbry at the other. Two vaulted cellars filled up the rest of the main block, and underneath the main stairway in the wing is another small vault, possibly used as a pit or prison. This main stair is a handsome squared scale-and-platt, which is unusual, and rises only to the first floor, above which the ascent is continued by the turret stair. The Hall, on the first floor, was a fine apartment, 27 by 17 feet, with a large fireplace in the east wall, the flue for which is carried up in the large chimney-stack which abuts the stair-turret. It has two mural chambers in the thick north gable, which contains the huge flue from the kitchen fireplace, and three small aumbries elsewhere. Above was the usual sleeping accommodation.

Sorbie appears to have been Church lands, under the nearby Candida Casa, the Abbey of Whithorn. Just when the first Hannays came to Sorbie is not clear; they may have been Church tenants. There are claims for a very early connection, even as early as the 13th century. As to documentary evidence, Patrick

[231]

Ahannay of Sorbie transmitted various lands to his son between 1529 and 1539. By 1612 John Ahannay was of Sorbie, and he was still laird in 1638. Patrick Hannay, the well-known poet, was of this family, and was also general of artillery to Gustavus Adolphus. The Hannays were much at feud with the Murrays of Broughton (not to be confused with the Peebles-shire house of that name) and in 1601 they were put to the horn for this fighting. This feud, and the heavy costs suffered by them in the Civil War, forced them to sell Sorbie to the Earl of Galloway in the 1670s. The Stewarts of Galloway were, however, linked to the Hannays by marriage. The last of the Sorbie Stewarts died in 1748, when the castle was allowed to fall into ruin.

Now, happily, it has become the property of the Clan Hannah Society which has plans for at least partial restoration.

## SORNHILL, AYRSHIRE

This is a tall and attractive laird's house of the 17th century, now a farmhouse, standing on the high ground about two miles south-east of Galston, above the Galston-Sorn road. It is an L-planned building of three storeys and a garret, with steep roofs and crow-stepped gables, having a square stair-tower rising in the re-entrant angle. This ends in a gabled watch-chamber a storey higher than the main roofing, which has its own fireplace and chimney. The walls are roughcast and yellow-washed, covering any details of the masonry. There is an unsightly modern porch at the foot of the stair-tower, covering the original entrance. The windows,

where they have not been enlarged, are small, and have simple roll mouldings, a number being built up. There is an empty panel space above porch and doorway, and quite a plethora of inscribed lintels to windows thereabouts, these being badly weatherworn and indecipherable; but one above the first floor window shows the date 16?? and another on a small staircase window seems to bear the initials N.M.R. or K.

It was not possible to see the interior of the house, which apparently has been largely modernised within. The ground floor is not vaulted now, if ever it was.

The lands of Sornhill, which lie only about half a mile south of the important castle of Cessnock, long the seat of the great Campbell of Cessnock family, related to the Loudoun earldom, almost inevitably came into the hands of that house. In 1553 we read that Mariota Nisbet, with the consent of her husband John Lockhart of Barr, sold lands of Sornhill to Sir Hugh Campbell of Loudoun. There was a noted and ancient family of Nisbet of Greenholm in this parish; and Barr Castle, the Lockhart's seat, still stands in the little town of Galston. This John Lockhart was a zealous reformer, and Knox preached in his house in 1556. In 1670 Barr was also sold to the Campbells. The present house of Sornhill dates from considerably after 1553 however.


# THREAVE CASTLE, KIRKCUDBRIGHTSHIRE

This famous stronghold, noted seat of the Black Douglas family, is especially interesting; for its renown; its massive bulk; its extraordinary site on an island of the River Dee, unapproachable by any bridge; and the fact that unlike most such castles it belongs almost entirely to one period, the 14th century. It stands in the marshy plain of the Dee about a mile west of Castle Douglas, and is not the most accessible of monuments even now, what with a longish walk and the ferry-boat passage.

The plan is simple, a great oblong keep of five storeys and formerly a garret, surrounded by a curtain-walled courtyard with circular flanking-towers at the four angles, only that to the south-east remaining. Beyond these walls was a ditch and rampart, to three sides, the river running close on the west; and formerly an enclosed forecourt. A fine gateway has pierced the curtain-wall at the east side, giving access to the inner court.

The keep, with walls 8 feet in thickness, rises 70 feet to the flush parapet. The masonry is the local small rubble with free-

stone dressings, of a reddish hue. The windows are fairly large for the period. Just below parapet-level there are three long rows of beam-holes, cut in the north, south and east sides, for the support of a projecting timber gallery or *bretâche*, for the better defence of the walling, a feature not often seen in surviving Scots castles, although many must have had such defensive aids. The west side, overlooking the river, was evidently not considered to require such.

The entrance to the castle has been, as usual, at the first or mezzanine floor, on the east side, formerly reached by a removable timber bridge from the gatehouse in the curtain-wall. This floor is really only the upper, or entresol, half of the high basement vault, and has been used as a kitchen, with a 10-foot wide fireplace and a sink formed in a window-embrasure. From here was reached the ground floor chamber, dimly lit by slits and containing a well, a stone sink and drain, and four recesses. A deep dungeon or pit has been contrived at the north-west corner, reached by a trap from above.

A small wheel-stair, projecting somewhat inwardly, rises from the entrance floor. On the first main floor was the Great Hall, a fine apartment measuring 46 by 25 feet, with fireplace and an angled garderobe. There was formerly access from here, by bridge, to the upper part of the gatehouse and the parapet of the perimeter wall, corbels for the support of which remain. The second floor is similar, with more elaborate fireplace. The storey above is particularly well-lit with ten windows. There have been mural passages at this level for the installing of the timbers for the *bretâche*. There are also corbels for a defensive machicolation high above the doorway.

Although the roof and garret storey and chimney-stacks have gone, and the parapet is now fragmentary, the remains still give an impressive indication of the original aspect. The building is now in the care of the Ministry of Works.

The builder was the famous Archibald the Grim, 3rd Earl of Douglas natural son of Bruce's friend, the Good Sir James, who was granted the Lordship of Galloway in 1369. His son's widow, sister of James the First, the Duchess of Touraine, resided here, and saw her unfortunate teenage sons, the 6th Earl and his brother, ride from Threave to the infamous Black Dinner at Edinburgh Castle in 1440, to their murder by Crichton and Livingstone. The castle was inherited by their sister, the renowned Fair Maid of Galloway, who, marrying her cousin, William 8th Earl, reunited the family, and Threave entered its most brilliant period, with that illustrious character dominating Scotland until his own assassination by James the Second at Stirling. Here was the base for many raids on England, and here was beheaded Maclellan of Bombie, in defiance of the King's command. James besieged the murdered Earl's brothers here, using heavy artillery, allegedly the famed Mons Meg. Thereafter Threave became a royal fortress, forming part of the jointure of successive queens. Arran besieged it in 1545, and the Earl of Nithsdale garrisoned it for King Charles in 1639-40. The Covenant leaders eventually dismantled it; but it was still fit for use as a gaol for French prisoners in the early 19th century.

## TORWOOD CASTLE, STIRLINGSHIRE

This is a handsome and commodious fortalice of the second half of the 16th century, long ruinous but with the main features surviving. It stands on high ground about two miles north of Larbert, half a mile west of the main A9 road, with the remains of the ancient and historic Tor Wood close by. It is an L-planned building, which has had a courtyard to the north, with 17th-century outbuildings, now largely gone. The structure consists of a long main block of three storeys lying east and west, with a stair-wing projecting northwards at the west end and rising two storeys higher, to house the usual gabled watch-chamber. Within the re-entrant angle rises also a square stair-tower—not the more usual corbelled stair-turret—and this appears to have stopped short a storey lower than the wing. A tiny corbelled-out circular turret, only part remaining, carried the stair to the watch-chamber. The

masonry is good throughout and well supplied with shot-holes and gunloops. There is a slight projection of the main block gable at the south-west corner, to provide flanking cover of the wall, defensively. The south face of the house is exceedingly plain, but the entrance front, to the north, compensates, with pleasing features and decorative work, including a stringcourse at first-floor level round wing and tower, and an empty panel space above the door.

The moulded doorway in the re-entrant, is guarded by gun-loops and a long slot for a draw-bar, and has a relieving arch above. The door admits to a lobby from which rises the main turnpike stair. A narrow guardroom is contrived in the wing gable, to the right. From the lobby a long vaulted passage opens along the north side of the main block, from which three cellars and the kitchen are reached, all vaulted, the kitchen being at the far east end. This is provided with the usual wide arched fireplace, a water inlet and a service hatch into the corridor. There is a tiny chamber off, to the north-east for purpose uncertain. The western-most basement chamber is the wine-cellar, with the usual private stair to the Hall above. There is also a small square room off, in the foot of the western projection.

Half-way up the main stair there is a vestibule contrived, with basin and drain. Higher is the Hall, a large apartment, 41 by 22 feet, having a decorative fireplace in the north wall, and a with-drawing-room off at the east end. This last has two tiny chambers hollowed out of the thick east gable, which houses the kitchen flue, and these have low ceilings, above which are windows to light the main withdrawing-room—an unusual arrangement. The upper floor, reached by the smaller stair in the stair-tower, is now ruinous, but has had dormer windows.

The courtyard, entered by a pend to the north, was extensive, and has a vaulted well-chamber at the north-east angle.

The family of Forester of Garden, taking their name from the office of keepers of the royal forest of Tor Wood, were the lairds here from the 15th century, although the present castle appears to have been built about 1566—a carved stone to that effect being preserved in Falkirk Museum. In the 17th century the lands passed to the Forresters of Corstorphine, and it was probably this family who built the courtyard extensions. In Tor Wood, so famous strategically and as a shelter for hiding men, this castle must have seen many stirring events.

# WOODHALL, EAST LOTHIAN

Giving an impression of remoteness, in the pleasant rolling wood-land country about a mile west of Pencaitland, this small mansion incorporates a tower of the 16th century, which has been restored in 1884, in process of which the roof-level has been somewhat lowered. It is a simple construction, oblong on plan, with walls of good local coursed rubble 4 feet in thickness, now rising only to two storeys, with a gabled roof and crowsteps, less steep than heretofore, and a semi-circular angle-turret projecting at the north-east corner, the upper courses of which have been renewed. There have been outer works, no doubt walling to enclose a courtyard, to east and south, possibly with a flanking-tower and ditching.

The entrance is now through the modern house at the west corner of the south wall, a slantwise opening slapped through to the vaulted basement chamber. This was the kitchen, measuring 19 by 13 feet, with fireplace in the south gable, and two windows, now much enlarged, facing east. The original entrance may have been at first-floor level, although this is not usual in a late 16th-century house. Or there may possibly have been a wing to the south-west, making the plan L-shaped. The house has been modernised internally, making assessment of the original arrange-ments difficult. It is now in excellent condition and appreciatively maintained.

Woodhall was part of the barony of Wester Pencaitland. Early included in the great lands of the Seton family, to whom all these territories were granted by the triumphant Bruce to his sister's

son, Woodhall passed in 1488 to John Sinclair of Hermanston nearby, of 'the lordly line of high St. Clair', collaterals of the great Orkney and Roslin house. In 1644 the property was resigned in favour of Robert Sinclair of Longformacus, and remained in possession of this line until the 18th century. In 1799, however, the castle was in ruins, and the 19th-century restoration was evidently only of a portion of the whole. The Lauders thereafter acquired the estate.

# MUCH-ALTERED STRUCTURES

A LIST, by no means exhaustive, of fortified houses which, although dating in some part from the defensive period, and surviving, have been so altered at a later period, as to leave little of the earlier work visible, or to offer a wholly different appearance. These buildings are extra to previous lists.

Aldourie Castle, Inverness-shire
Ardchattan House, Argyll
Old House of Borgue, Kirkcudbrightshire
Bunchrew House, Inverness-shire
Darnaway Castle, Moray
Foulis Castle, Ross
Old House of Gask, Perthshire
Gordon Castle, Moray
Gordonstoun House, Moray
Hempriggs House, Caithness
Inshes House, Inverness-shire
Kilberry Castle, Argyll
Letterfourie House, Banffshire
Logie Almond House, Perthshire
Milton Brodie, Moray
Milton Keith, Banffshire
Rait Castle, Nairnshire.

Milton Keith

# INDEX

[244]

# COMPLETE ALPHABETICAL LIST OF BUILDINGS DESCRIBED IN THE FIVE VOLUMES

Aberdour Castle, 2
Abergeldie Castle, 4
Aberuchill Castle, 2
Aboyne Castle, 4
Achanachie Castle, 4
Ackergill Tower, 5
Affleck (or Auchinleck) Castle, 4
Aiket Castle, 3
Airdrie House, 2
Airlie Castle, 4
Airth Castle, 2
Aldbar Castle, 4
Alderston House, 1
Aldie Castle, 2
Allardyce Castle, 4
Alloa Tower, 2
Amisfield Tower, 3
Anstruther Easter Manse, 2
Ardblair Castle, 2
Ardmillan Castle, 3
Arnage Castle, 4
Ascog House, 5
Ashintully Castle, 2
Aswanley House, 4
Auchans Castle, 3
Auchenbowie House, 2
Auchenvole Castle, 2
Auchness Castle, 3

Balbegno Castle, 4
Balbithan House, 4
Balcomie Castle, 2
Balfluig Castle, 4
Balfour Castle, 4
Balgone Castle, 2
Ballindalloch Castle, 5
Ballone Castle, 5
Balmanno Castle, 2

Balmuto House, 2
Balnagown Castle, 5
Balnakeil House, 5
Baltersan Castle, 3
Balthayock Castle, 2
Balvaird Castle, 2
Balvenie Castle, 5
Bamff House, 2
Barcaldine Castle, 2
Bardowie Castle, 2
Barholm Castle, 3
Barjarg Tower, 3
Barmagachan, 3
Barncluith, 3
Barns Tower, 1
Barr Castle (Ayr), 3
Barr Castle (Renfrew), 3
Barra Castle, 4
Barscobe Castle, 3
Bavelaw Castle, 1
Bedlay House, 3
Bedlormie House, 5
Beldorney Castle, 4
Belmont Castle, 2
Bemersyde, 1
Benholm Tower, 4
Bishops' House, Elgin, 5
Bishopton House, 3
Blair Castle (Ayr), 3
Blair Castle (Perth), 2
Blairfindy Castle, 5
Blairlogie Castle, 2
Blervie Castle, 5
Bonhard House, 1
Bonshaw Tower, 3
Borthwick Castle, 1
Braco Castle, 2
Braemar Castle, 4
Braikie Castle, 4
Branxholme Castle, 1
Breachacha Castle, 5

Breckonside Tower, 3
Bridge Castle, 1
Brims Castle, 5
Brodick Castle, 5
Brodie Castle, 5
Broughty Castle, 4
Brunstane House, 5
Bruntsfield House, 1
Buckholm Tower, 1
Buittle Place, 3
Burnhead Tower, 1
Burgie Castle, 5
Burleigh Castle, 2

Cadboll Castle, 5
Caerlaverock Castle, 5
Cairnbulg Castle, 4
Cairnhill or Carnell, 3
Cakemuir Castle, 1
Calder House, 1
Caldwell Tower, 3
Campbell, Castle, 2
Carberry Tower, 1
Cardoness Castle, 3
Cardross House, 2
Careston Castle, 4
Carnasserie Castle, 5
Carrick Castle, 5
Carriden House, 1
Carse Gray, 4
Carsluith Castle, 3
Cassillis House, 3
Castlecary, 2
Castlemilk, 3
Cavers House, 5
Cawdor Castle, 5
Cessnock Castle, 3
Clackmannan Tower, 2
Claypotts Castle, 4
Cleish Castle, 2

## Date Due

| Date | Due | | |
|---|---|---|---|
| FEB 25 1972 | | | |
| NOV 2 8 1978 | | | |
| SEP 1 9 1990 | | | |
| APR 2 5 1991 | | | |
| K088 259 | | | |
| 2-12 | | | |
| SEP 0 8 199 | | | |
| JAN 1 7 199 | | | |
| | | | |
| | | | |
| | | | |
| | | | |
| | | | |
| | | | |
| | | | |